3D Game Design with Unreal Engine 4 and Blender

Combine the powerful UE4 with Blender to create visually appealing and comprehensive game environments

Justin Plowman

[PACKT] open source *
PUBLISHING   community experience distilled

BIRMINGHAM - MUMBAI

3D Game Design with Unreal Engine 4 and Blender

First published: June 2016

Production reference: 1240616

Published by Packt Publishing Ltd.
Livery Place
35 Livery Street
Birmingham B3 2PB, UK.

ISBN 978-1-78588-146-6

www.packtpub.com

Credits

Author
Justin Plowman

Reviewer
Scott Hafner

Commissioning Editor
Amarabha Banerjee

Acquisition Editor
Rahul Nair

Content Development Editor
Parshva Sheth

Technical Editor
Gebin George

Copy Editor
Safis Editing

Project Coordinator
Ritika Manoj

Proofreader
Safis Editing

Indexer
Monica Ajmera Mehta

Graphics
Disha Haria

Production Coordinator
Arvindkumar Gupta

Cover Work
Arvindkumar Gupta

About the Author

Justin Plowman is a game designer and educator, who resides in the United States. At a young age, he discovered his love for video games and the joy they bring to others. He began teaching high school students about game development in 2005 and enjoys supporting the dreams of the next generation developers. He currently teaches at risk youth about game design and development through the West Michigan Center for Arts and Technology (www.wmcat.org); and also teaches Unreal Engine development as part of the Digital Animation and Game Design program at Ferris State University (www.ferris.edu). Justin has worked with Unreal Technology in the education arena for more than 10 years. When not teaching, he writes learning tutorials on different topics related to Unreal Technology, and continues to further his education by keeping up on recent industry news and learning about best practices related to both teaching and game development. He can be found on the Web at https://gamingbootcamp.wordpress.com/.

Writing this book has been quite a journey for me, as it firmly falls in the realm of the things that I never expected to do. However, it has truly been a rewarding experience, and I can't thank the folks at *Packt Publishing* enough for this opportunity. I want to thank my wife, Jennifer, for helping me focus through the long nights of writing and development, as well as my good friend, Jacob Pollak, for providing me with the amazing piece of cover art. Most of all, I would like to thank the great Unreal Engine online community that has been instrumental in growing and nurturing my skills over the years. This book represents my desire to give back, and I hope that it encourages more designers and developers within the community to do the same. Thank you!

About the Reviewer

Scott Hafner is a professional game designer with over 10 years of experience in the video game industry. Over the course of his career, Scott has worked as a producer, a game designer, and a level designer on a range of platforms and genres including MMOs, third-person shooters, and RPGs.

I would like to thank my wife for her continued encouragement and support in all that I do!

www.PacktPub.com

eBooks, discount offers, and more

Did you know that Packt offers eBook versions of every book published, with PDF and ePub files available? You can upgrade to the eBook version at `www.PacktPub.com` and as a print book customer, you are entitled to a discount on the eBook copy. Get in touch with us at `customercare@packtpub.com` for more details.

At `www.PacktPub.com`, you can also read a collection of free technical articles, sign up for a range of free newsletters and receive exclusive discounts and offers on Packt books and eBooks.

`https://www2.packtpub.com/books/subscription/packtlib`

Do you need instant solutions to your IT questions? PacktLib is Packt's online digital book library. Here, you can search, access, and read Packt's entire library of books.

Why subscribe?

- Fully searchable across every book published by Packt
- Copy and paste, print, and bookmark content
- On demand and accessible via a web browser

Table of Contents

Preface

With an explosive growth in independent game development in the last few years, many developers are looking for robust and low-cost tools that would enable them to bring their dream games to market.

Blender is a powerful open source 3D software package used by developers across the globe; it is renowned for its ease of use and active community. Unreal Engine 4 is the amazing AAA game engine built by Epic Games that has become the go to choice for many game developers, large and small.

During the course of this book, we will look at how to utilize Blender to create both animated and static game art for Unreal Engine 4 and how to bring these assets into our own projects.

What this book covers

Chapter 1, Unreal, My Friend, I'd Like You to Meet Blender, will guide you through installing and setting up the Blender 3D software package. We will discuss Blender's interface and tools as well as get started on our first project.

Chapter 2, Starting Our First Project, takes us into Unreal Engine 4 to begin designing the first level of our project. We will review some level design basics and put together a game level for our future game art to exist in.

Chapter 3, It's Time to Customize!, will have us started on creating the first game asset in Blender—a space age crate for our cargo ship level. We will cover basic modeling techniques and discuss the process for UV unwrapping and texturing our game asset.

Chapter 4, Getting the Assets to the Level, will discuss the process of exporting our crate from Blender and importing it into Unreal so that we can utilize it within our cargo ship level.

Chapter 5, Taking This Level Up a Notch, will see us move on from the cargo ship to building a space station level, with complete scripted events to add emotions for the player's experience. We will take a look at more advanced scripting techniques in Blueprint and prepare our level to receive a more advanced game asset.

Chapter 6, Monster Assets – The Level Totally Needs One of These, takes us through the design process to create a more advanced game asset—the Artifact. We will take a look at several more 3D modeling tools, and you will understand how to build your game asset from multiple components.

Chapter 7, Let's Dress to Impress, takes us through the process of UV unwrapping all the different pieces that make up the Artifact. We will look at some advanced UV tools in Blender. You will also learn how to utilize Substance Painter to create some amazing textures and materials.

Chapter 8, Lights, Camera, Animation!, brings us back to Blender to create animations for the Artifact. We will discuss the requirements for bringing animations into Unreal Engine 4, as well as using bones and rigging in Blender.

Chapter 9, Bang Bang – Let's Make It Explode, ends the book with a look at creating video game explosions using sound, particle effects, and flying parts. We will celebrate the completion of our game asset by importing it to Unreal Engine 4 and setting it to explode!

What you need for this book

The following hardware and software are needed for this book:

- Desktop PC or Mac
- Windows 7 64-bit or Mac OS X 10.10 or later
- Quad-core Intel or AMD processor, 2.5 GHz, or faster
- NVIDIA GeForce 470 GTX or AMD Radeon 6870 HD series card or a higher version
- 8 GB RAM
- A three-button mouse
- Unreal Engine 4.9 or a later version
- Blender 2.76 Release Candidate 3 or a later version
- Substance Painter 1.7 30 day free trial or a later version

All software mentioned in this book is free of charge and can be downloaded from the Internet.

Who this book is for

This book is ideal for 3D artists and game designers who want to create amazing 3D game environments and leverage the power of Blender with Unreal Engine 4. 3D design basics would be necessary to get the most out of this book. Some previous experience with Blender would be helpful but not essential.

Conventions

In this book, you will find a number of text styles that distinguish between different kinds of information. Here are some examples of these styles and an explanation of their meaning.

Code words in text, database table names, folder names, filenames, file extensions, pathnames, dummy URLs, user input, and Twitter handles are shown as follows: "This can be found by typing Input E into the Find a Node search box."

New terms and **important words** are shown in bold. Words that you see on the screen, for example, in menus or dialog boxes, appear in the text like this: "Click on the **Add Modifier** dropdown and select **Mirror**."

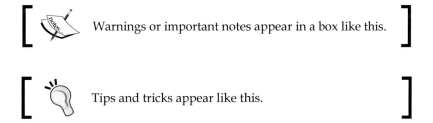

Warnings or important notes appear in a box like this.

Tips and tricks appear like this.

Reader feedback

Feedback from our readers is always welcome. Let us know what you think about this book—what you liked or disliked. Reader feedback is important for us as it helps us develop titles that you will really get the most out of.

To send us general feedback, simply e-mail feedback@packtpub.com, and mention the book's title in the subject of your message.

If there is a topic that you have expertise in and you are interested in either writing or contributing to a book, see our author guide at www.packtpub.com/authors.

Customer support

Now that you are the proud owner of a Packt book, we have a number of things to help you to get the most from your purchase.

Downloading the color images of this book

We also provide you with a PDF file that has color images of the screenshots/diagrams used in this book. The color images will help you better understand the changes in the output. You can download this file from `https://www.packtpub.com/sites/default/files/downloads/3DGameDesignwithUnrealEngine4andBlender_coloredImages.pdf`.

Errata

Although we have taken every care to ensure the accuracy of our content, mistakes do happen. If you find a mistake in one of our books—maybe a mistake in the text or the code—we would be grateful if you could report this to us. By doing so, you can save other readers from frustration and help us improve subsequent versions of this book. If you find any errata, please report them by visiting `http://www.packtpub.com/submit-errata`, selecting your book, clicking on the **Errata Submission Form** link, and entering the details of your errata. Once your errata are verified, your submission will be accepted and the errata will be uploaded to our website or added to any list of existing errata under the Errata section of that title.

To view the previously submitted errata, go to `https://www.packtpub.com/books/content/support` and enter the name of the book in the search field. The required information will appear under the **Errata** section.

Piracy

Piracy of copyrighted material on the Internet is an ongoing problem across all media. At Packt, we take the protection of our copyright and licenses very seriously. If you come across any illegal copies of our works in any form on the Internet, please provide us with the location address or website name immediately so that we can pursue a remedy.

Please contact us at `copyright@packtpub.com` with a link to the suspected pirated material.

We appreciate your help in protecting our authors and our ability to bring you valuable content.

Questions

If you have a problem with any aspect of this book, you can contact us at
questions@packtpub.com, and we will do our best to address the problem.

1
Unreal, My Friend, I'd Like You to Meet Blender

As game developers, all of us have our dream game—that one game that excites us and sticks in our minds no matter how many years have passed. For some, that means waiting until another game developer builds something like it, but their version never quite matches up with our own. For most of us, the desire to see this game made and to be able to play it became the catalyst for starting our careers in independent game development. As we build our dreams and pour our heart and souls into the development of games, we still want to compete with the big boys in today's game markets, but we don't have the money for commercial licenses of "triple A" game engines and high-end 3D software packages. That all changed a few years ago when big 3D game engines like **Unreal Engine** went free for indie developers. Now smaller developers have the same access to high-end tools that larger developers enjoy. These new game engines gave us the ability to build the games of our dreams. However, 3D art programs never really followed suit. Many of the industry standard creation suites, such as **Autodesk 3ds Max**, still cost thousands of dollars. This changed in 2002 with the creation of the **Blender Foundation**, a nonprofit organization dedicated to the support of Blender. Blender is an open source 3D creation software that allows small developers like us to use our art in our commercial projects without having to spend tons of money up front. We can finally create the 3D games of our dreams without the stress of having to wonder how we can pay for the tools we need.

And that's why you're here. Maybe you are already an independent developer using the latest version of Unreal Engine 4, but are still only using game assets created by others. Maybe you are a complete novice with your mind filled with amazing digital vistas that need to be created. Either way, this book is for you. Within these pages, we will take a look at how to use Blender and Unreal Engine 4 together to create custom levels and game content for your games.

In this chapter, we will cover the following topics:

- Installing Blender
- Exploring the interface
- Customizing your settings
- Working with modes
- Jumping into our first project
- Getting things started in Unreal Engine 4

Installing Blender

The first step along our development journey begins at http://www.blender.org, online home of the Blender Foundation. Here you can learn about the history of Blender, connect with their community, access training videos, and more. I encourage you to check out the website when you have time as it has much to offer. For example, every time there is a major update to the software, there is also a release of an animated short film. These films tend to be very entertaining as well as show what the toolset is capable of.

Here's how you download Blender:

1. Go to http://www.blender.org/.
2. Click on the button on the right labeled **Download Blender 2.76-rc3** (the current version as of this writing):

Click the download button to get the latest version of Blender

3. Blender is a cross-platform software. Select a 64- or 32-bit mirror for your operating system. Most likely, your computer will be 64 bit:

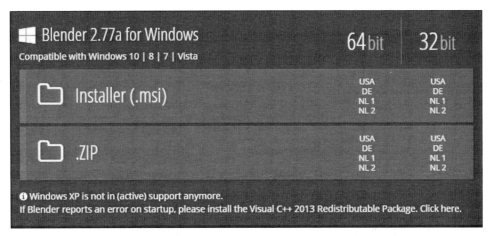

Click the download link that is closest to your location and that corresponds to your operating system. Most users will need the 64 bit version, but if you have less than 8 gigs of RAM you should use the 32 bit version

4. Click on the **Installer** once it has finished downloading.

5. Follow the installation prompts. They are pretty straightforward and do not need additional configuration.

Once everything has been installed, go ahead and run the program. You will be greeted with the splash screen. Now let's take a look at the interface.

Exploring the interface

When you run Blender, you are greeted by the splash screen. A list of files you have worked on recently will be listed on the left, as well as some quick links to various things, such as the documentation and the website. Click in the space to either side of the splash screen to remove it. Now let's take a look at the default scene.

Blender starts you off with three basic objects in the scene already: a cube, a light, and a camera, as shown in the following screenshot:

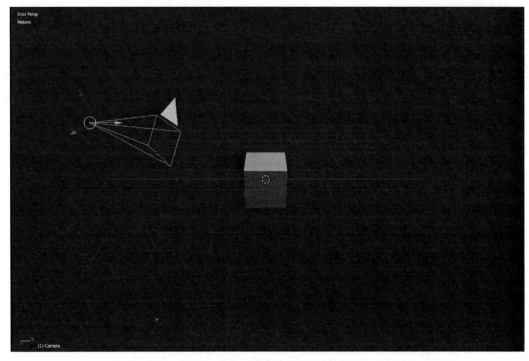

Our Blender default setup. We will change this to work better with Unreal 4

Select any one of them by right-clicking on the object. This will highlight it in orange. Try right-clicking on other objects in the scene:

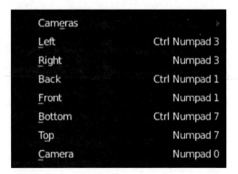

We can rotate our point of view around the center by holding the middle mouse button (*MMB*). We can slide our view by holding *Shift* + *MMB* and zoom it using the mouse wheel or + and - on the number pad. Lastly, the number pad can also be used to view specific angles of your object.

Now let's take a look at the menus:

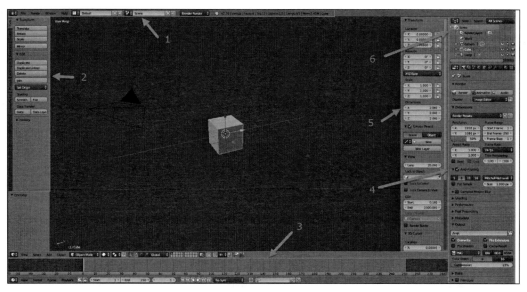

The Blender interface

1. Menu Bar
2. Tools Panel
3. Animation Timeline
4. Properties
5. Scene Properties (press N if you don't see this menu)
6. Scene Outliner

All of the preceding options have several functions. We will discuss them briefly here and more as we continue with the project:

- **Menu Bar**: This contains the **File, Render, Window, Help, Scene Layout** drop-down, **Browse Scene** drop-down, and the **Render Engine** drop-down options. For the most part, we will use the **File** menu to save, load, change user preferences, export our files, and exit the program.

- **Tools Panel**: This contains most of our functions that we will use to edit our shapes and mold our creations.

- **Animation Timeline**: We will use this later to manage our animated game asset.

- **Properties**: We will use the panel frequently to edit the properties of our scene, add modifiers, and more.

- **Scene Properties**: This contains a few specific functions that pertain to items in the scene, such as scale.

- **Scene Outliner**: This is a convenient list of every object in our scene and is handy if you can't find a specific object visually. Unreal Engine has one of these as well.

A lot of information, huh? Trust me, it gets easier with practice. To make things even easier, let's customize some of our settings.

Customizing your settings

Without customizing some of your settings, working with Blender can be a bit of a chore, especially if you have any experience with another 3D software. When we started moving around the interface a bit, you may have noticed right away that if you left-click, it moves the little bullseye cursor. This is called the 3D cursor and it is actually used for a lot of things within Blender, such as where to place new 3D shapes. Now, moving this when you left-click is less than ideal and is sometimes easily forgotten as you attempt to select things in your 3D scene, but there is a way to change that.

In the top-left corner of the screen, click on **File** and select **User Preferences**. Select the **Input** tab and look down along the left-hand side until you see the **Select With** option. You can see that it's currently set to right-click to select objects. Let's change that to **Left** to bring it more in line with Unreal Engine 4. It stops a lot of confusion later when you are going between the two programs. Be sure to click on the **Save User Settings** button at the bottom left corner once you have made this change. The second setting that needs to be changed involves scale.

The following screenshot shows the **Blender User Preferences** window:

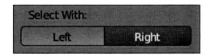

Setting the mouse selection to use the LMB

To change this next setting, we are going to take a look at the **Properties** pane. The window looks something like this:

Along the top of the pane are several small tabs. We are looking for the **Scene** tab denoted by this icon:

Setting the mouse selection to use the LMB

This pane allows us to change several options pertaining to the scene, such as the scale. Unreal Engine 4 uses centimeters as its default measurement, so we want to match that here. This will make our game assets fit into our levels without the need to scale them in the game engine. Follow these steps:

1. Change the units used from **None** to **Metric**.
2. Change the scale to 0.01.
3. Objects already in the scene (such as our cube) will not scale. If there is anything you would like to keep, scale it by 100. This can be done by clicking on the **Scale** button on the left hand side, typing 100, and pressing *Enter*.
4. This will cause the object to start clipping through the edge of the grid. To fix this, we press *N* to open the **Scene Properties** bar, find the **View** section, then the **Clip** section, and lastly, change the **End** property to 1km.

 Hint: Certain objects dropped in through the **Add** menu will not be scaled appropriately. Scaling these objects by 100 will fix the issue.

Now that we have made those changes, save your file by using the **File** menu or pressing *Ctrl + S*.

Working with modes

Blender has one more menu we haven't talked about yet. This is a small menu bar along the bottom of the 3D view that looks like the following:

The menu bar at the bottom of the 3d view. We will use this a lot!

It contains the **View**, **Select**, **Add**, and **Object** menus. It also contains the modes drop-down. We will use many different modes throughout this book, but we will spend most of our time in the **Edit** mode. This mode allows us to push and pull basic shapes into our new creations. Blender allows us to switch between **Object** mode (the default mode) and **Edit** mode fairly easily by pressing *Tab*. This will only work if you have an object that can be edited selected in the scene. You will notice that many of the menus change when you change modes. We will explore this more when we create our first object in *Chapter 3, It's Time to Customize!*.

Hint: It may seem like I am skipping a bunch of information. Blender's menus contain way more than I can explain in one chapter of this book and I don't want to bog you down with unnecessary information. If you are curious, check out *Blender 3D Basics Beginner's Guide*, Second Edition, by Gordon Fisher, for a more complete description.

Jumping into our first project

This book is broken into two projects that will have us creating custom game assets in Blender and adding them to levels built in Unreal Engine 4. The first project will be a basic level that I have taught many students to create over my 10 years of teaching experience: two rooms connected by a hallway with some stairs, doors that function, and an elevator. Though the level itself is not complicated, we will walk through the entire design process from idea, to prototype, to the final product. We will then use this same process to design a more complex level later in this book. The levels themselves will be created with a science fiction horror theme in mind. Having a theme will unite the two levels and give us an art style to work with when the time comes to design custom level assets.

So how do you design a level from scratch? Our process will follow a few distinct steps:

1. Every good thing starts on paper. Artists start ideas with sketches. Architects have blueprints. Level designers start their levels with map sketches. I recommend graph paper. We will start our custom game assets with sketches as well.

2. Begin laying out the level using basic shapes in your level editor. Script gameplay sequences. Test the level to see if the layout works for the player. This is called white boxing, or boxing out your level. It is essentially a level prototype.

3. Once your white box level is where you would like it, use the blocked out sizes to begin creating and adding game assets. This allows us to make assets in Blender that are of the correct size and fill the correct space in our level.

4. Add in your game assets, adjust lighting, and add special effects.

5. Don't forget to playtest and gather the opinions of your players every step of the way!

Now let's get our project started in Unreal Engine 4.

Getting things started in Unreal Engine 4

Before we get started with Unreal, make sure that you have installed the **Epic Games Launcher**. This is available for free at `https://www.UnrealEngine.com/` and can be downloaded by clicking on the **Get Unreal** button located at the top right-hand corner of the page. You will be asked to create an account and the launcher will ask for this information when you run it.

Next, click on the **Library** button along the left-hand side of the screen. In the section labeled **Engine** versions, click on **Launch** on version 4.9.2 (the latest version as of this writing). If there are no engines visible, select **Add Versions** and follow the prompts:

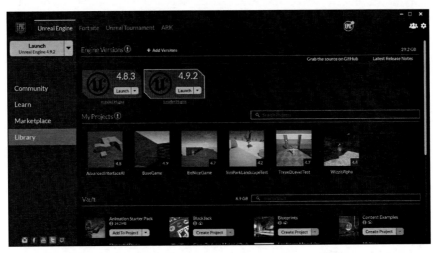

The Epic Games Launcher. Clicking Library on the Unreal Engine tab will show what engine version you have, as well as your current projects

Once the engine has loaded, you will be presented with all of the projects you have been working on. For this one, let's start a new project. Click on the **New Project** tab at the top, as shown in the following screenshot:

The New Projects tab

At this point, Unreal provides you with a few choices. The engine comes with many free starter projects to get you started on a number of different types of projects. For our projects, we will use the **First Person** starter project. Make sure that the **Starter Content** button says **With Starter Content** and give the project a unique name with no spaces. When you are all set, click on **Create Project,** down in the bottom right. Unreal Engine 4 will load and we will be all set to start our level.

Summary

Throughout this chapter, you took a look at the tools you will use to bring our level idea to life. Blender is a freely available open source creation suite that supports the entire asset development process. Created using the Python programming language, Blender is flexible enough to run on almost any machine and is entirely cross-platform; it runs in Windows, Mac, or Linux. Next, you took a look at the design process you will use and how Blender and Unreal Engine 4 plug into it. Lastly, you set up Unreal to begin our first project. As you move to the next chapter, you will build your first level that will play host to your first original game asset. Can you feel the excitement!?

2
Starting Our First Project

Now it's time for the exciting stuff! As we move forward with building our first project, we are going to use the design process we talked about in the last chapter and start with a level sketch. You might be tempted to just open up Unreal and jump right in, right? Why spend time drawing when I could be building that sweet level I've always wanted? Well, here's why. The best way to avoid multiple revisions and costly time spent redoing sections of your level is to plan in advance. Figure out the setting, architecture, background, and story of your level. Put some thought into where you will place story cues and power ups. Run your ideas by friends, players, and team members. Incorporate the feedback you receive and then build your level. It's the level designer's equivalent of "measure twice, cut once".

Let's take a look at our level sketch:

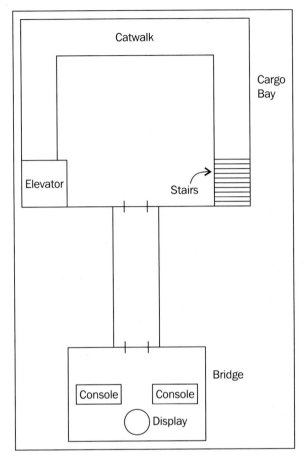

Our first level map!

So here is our first level. The level itself is pretty basic. We have two rooms connected by a hallway, with some stairs that lead up to a second tier. After we finish the basic layout, we can add a cargo elevator off to the side and working doors for the player to interact with. I have tried to lay out the level in the form of a small cargo ship, to fit the theme of our science fiction horror game. The level will function as an introduction to the setting, as well as a way to transport the player to the haunted space station environment we will be building later.

In this chapter, we will be covering the following topics:

* Building the level using Unreal's Content Browser
* Using different types of light

- Adding interactive elements using Triggers and Blueprints
- Playtesting our level

Using the Content Browser to start building the level

Go ahead and open **Epic Games Launcher**, and pull up the project we started at the end of the last chapter. Unreal Engine 4 was a huge upgrade over the last version of the engine, as it gave users a simple drag-and-drop interface. This was accomplished using two important panes in the interface: the **Modes** pane and the **Content Browser**. These portions of the interface allow level designers to drag elements into the level and place them where they need to go. Of these two, we will use the **Content Browser** the most:

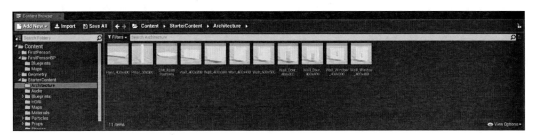

The Content Browser contains all of the game assets we will use

The **Content Browser** holds all of the objects, sounds, materials, and particles that can be used in your creation. These are sorted into folders that mirror the file structure where your project is stored. Unreal does this to make it easy to move project files around, should the need arise. Navigating the browser is easy. Double-clicking a folder opens that folder, while the top portion of the panel displays a breadcrumb trail that can be clicked on to move back through your selections. I like to ensure that the sources panel is on as well; this makes navigation and finding specific files easier. When we created our project, we told Unreal to include the **Starter Content** folder. This folder includes many basics for us to get started with, such as a variety of basic shapes, architecture pieces, materials, and more. With these, we can start whiteboxing our design.

Start by creating the first room:

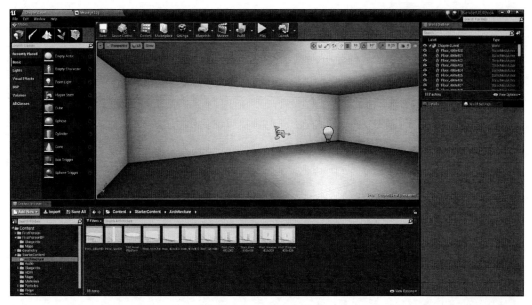

The first room of our project

Hint: Moving forward, we will begin building our level in Unreal. This book assumes the reader has a basic understanding of using Unreal Engine 4. If you are having issues following along, check out the *UnrealEngine* channel on YouTube for some great introductory tutorials from Epic Games. It can be found at `https://www.youtube.com/channel/UCBobmJyzsJ6Ll7UbfhI4iwQ/`.

To start building our first room, we are going to take advantage of the assets we have in the **Architecture** folder. Using its selection of floors, walls, and doors, we are going to assemble the first room of our design:

1. First let's start a new level in our project. Head up to the **File** menu, click it, and select new level. Choose **Empty Level** in the dialog box that appears.

2. The new level contains absolutely nothing. Perfect for our foray into space! Drop in a **Floor_400x400** piece as a place to start. This is done by clicking and dragging the piece into the level from the Content Browser. Head over to the details panel and make sure its location is set to `x=0 y=0 z=0`. This will make it easy to line up our other pieces.

3. Duplicate the floor five times. This can be easily done by holding *ALT* and moving the object to create a copy. Line them up in a 2x3 rectangle to create a good-sized room.

4. Next, let's grab some walls. Drag a **Wall_400x300** into the level, on top of one of your floor pieces:

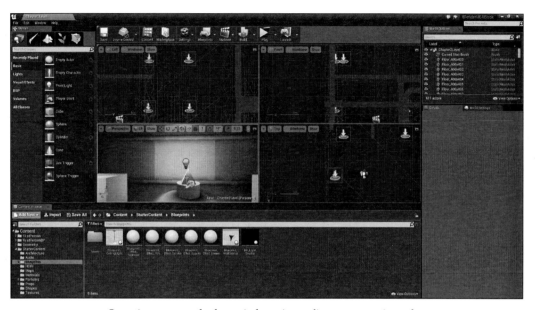

Sometimes we use the four window view to line up our static meshes

5. We are going to use the 4-viewport view to line up our wall section. In the top-right corner of your viewport, there is a row of icons, that control several different items such as grid snaps, angle snaps, scaling snaps, and camera speed. All the way over to the right of those icons is a minimize/maximize button. Click that to bring up your four viewports. Using two of those viewports, line up your wall section with a corner of your floor.

6. Copy the wall section and use the **Move** and **Rotate** tools to enclose the space.

7. Lastly, enclose the space by taking floor pieces and using them as a roof to complete the room.

At this point, I'm sure you are just dying to drop into the level and run around inside your new room. However, to test our level, we need to add a couple of things: lights and a player start. For testing purposes, let's drop in a couple of **PointLights**. Head over to the **Modes** panel on the left-hand side of the screen and drag two **PointLights** into your room. Again, use the 4-viewport configuration to make sure they are where you want them to be. Secondly, from the same panel, drag in a **PlayerStart**. The **PlayerStart** has an arrow sticking out from its center. That is what direction the player will be facing when they spawn. Always try to point your **PlayerStart** in the direction you want the player to go first. This ensures that the player is engaged from the start and can enjoy your creation with the minimum of confusion. Lastly, we need to save the file (using the **File** menu or *Ctrl + S*) and build the level using the **Build** button.

> The **Build** button bakes your lighting and finalizes all your level changes. This will give you the best idea of what your lighting looks like and is an essential part of testing game AI and other features. It's a good habit to build your level before testing.

Testing your level while it's being constructed is an important part of the design process. Through testing, you can discover if your level has any flaws or issues and fix them before things get too complicated. To test your level, press the **Play** button. This will start a play session in the current viewport and allow you to run around inside your level. If you click the little down arrow next to the **Play** button, you will be given the option to open other types of play windows, such as the **New Editor Window**. It can be helpful to be able to see the whole play screen. Now test your level and make sure everything is lined up properly. Once you feel good about your first room, let's build the rest of the design:

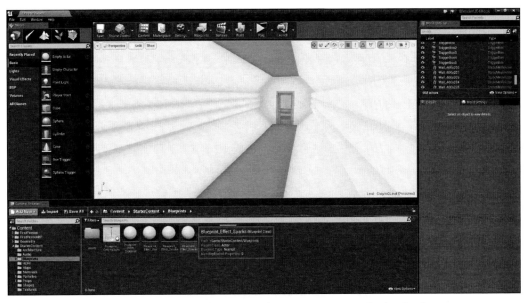

It is a good habit to add as much detail as you can to your whitebox level so
you have a good idea of what your design will look like

Now let's build the hallway. We can easily build out our hallway by copying existing
pieces in our level. I will also show you how to swap pieces in the level without
deleting them:

1. Select one of the floor pieces in your first room. Duplicate it and line it up
   with where you would like to place the doorway into the hallway space.

2. Go into the **Content Browser** and select **Wall_Door_400x300**. We are going to replace one of the wall sections with this piece. Now select the wall piece that you would like to replace in the viewport. Right-click on it and select **Replace Selected Actors with Wall_Door_400x300** from the menu:

Replacing our wall static mesh with a wall that contains a door

This will swap the existing static mesh with the one we selected and add in that perfect-sized doorway.

3. Copy the floor section twice more to lengthen the hallway. Don't forget to make sure all the pieces line up properly with your existing floor.

4. Copy a wall section and add it to your hallway. Copy that a few more times to enclose the length of your hallway.

5. Finally, copy the floor to create the ceiling and enclose your hallway, and add a light inside it.

 Remember that lights can be copied just like any other object. Another fast way to add a **PointLight** to your level is to hold the *L* key, then click where you would like the light to go.

Build your level and give it a test. If the hallway does not feel long enough, add a couple more sections. Once you are happy with the feel of your level so far, save your file. Now let's add the final room:

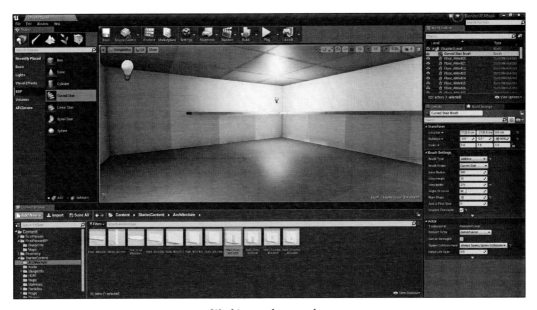

Working on the cargo bay

For this room, we will add some vertical elements to the design. We will also build both stairs and an elevator to access the walkways above, so let's begin:

1. As we have done for previous additions, let's copy a floor piece from the hallway and line it up with the doorway. This will be the start of our new room. This room will be larger than the last room, so let's copy our new floor section twice in each direction, creating a row of five floor pieces.

2. Now let's select all the floor pieces in that row by holding *Ctrl* and clicking on each piece. Copy this row four times to create our large room:

Creating the second story by duplicating the walls

3. Copy a wall section from the hallway into our room and use it to enclose the whole space, as we did in the hallway. Now select all of those wall pieces and copy them. Set those pieces on top of the originals to create a second floor:

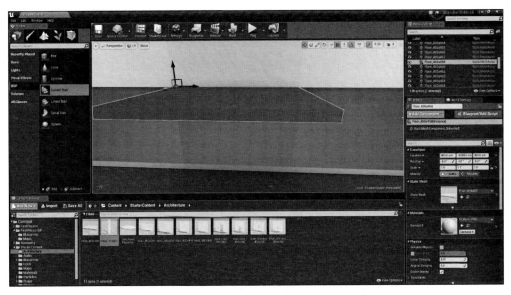

Duplicating the first floor section for the catwalk

4. Now let's create the catwalk for the second floor. Copy a floor piece toward the back of the room. Align it with the top of the wall.

5. Over in the **Details** panel, go over to **Scale** and type in 0.7 in the green box. This will scale our floor piece in the **Y** axis and decrease how wide our catwalk is:

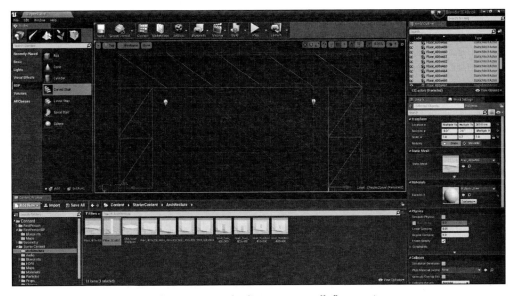

Using the top view to duplicate our catwalk floor sections

6. Copy our walkway piece around the outside of the room to create a U-shaped section. This will leave space for our stairs and elevator:

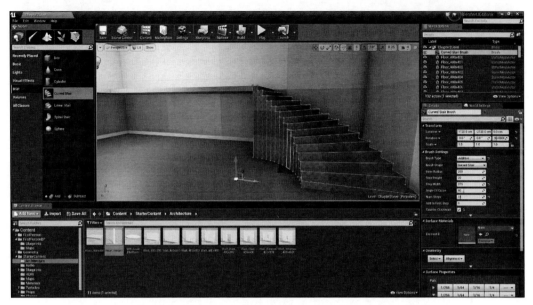

Creating the spiral staircase to give the player access to the second floor

7. Time for the stairs! Add in a **Curved Staircase** from the **BSP** menu in the Modes panel. Align it with our corner so that it will connect with our walkway. However, the default stairs aren't high enough. We can fix this by adding stairs in the **Details** panel and messing with the **Num Steps** option. We can adjust the size of our stairway by adjusting the **Step Width** option. The settings that worked for me were **Num Steps**: 15 and **Step Width**: 275.

8. Our last feature will be adding in the pieces we will need for our elevator:

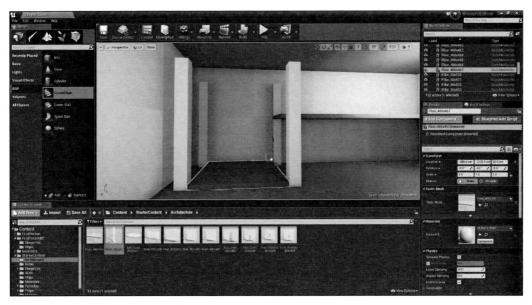

Starting to lay out our elevator components

For the elevator, I copied a floor piece and moved it to line up with my walkway above. I moved it up and down a few times to ensure it fit, before leaving it sitting on the floor in its down position. We will animate this piece to make the elevator work later in the chapter.

9. Grab a **Pillar_50x500** piece from the **Architecture** folder and arrange them around our elevator, and we are done.

Have you been working on this level on and off, and would like this level to open by default instead of the example? Go to the **Edit** menu and select **Project Settings**. Select **Maps & Modes** and change the **Game Default Map** and **Editor Starter Map** to your level file.

Now that we have our basic level geometry set inside the level, let's think about what other more decorative elements could be added to help reinforce the theme. Science fiction levels come in many different flavors. Some environments might be clean and simple, such as in the Star Trek universe. Others might be more industrial, with pipes and cabling everywhere, such as what we see in the Alien franchise. The aesthetics of a level can be used to reinforce the theme of an environment and communicate information to the player. In this case, we would like to reinforce the survival horror aspects. To do that, I will lean more toward an industrial style. Collecting reference art to help inspire your item placement can help you get the right feel and I strongly suggest taking a look at images online for some great examples. Remember that these props are just placeholders for art that can be created later. Ready? Let's get started with our first room:

1. Head on over to the **Shapes** folder within the **Starter Content** folder. This folder contains many basic shapes that will help approximate different props that could be created in Blender for this level.

2. Grab a **Shape_Cylinder** and drag it into the room. I envision this first room as being the bridge of our small cargo ship and the cylinder could serve as the hologram projector of a heads-up display for flying the ship. I added a **Shape_TriPyramid** on top of it and scaled that down a bit to make it look more techy.

3. Add in a couple of **Shape_Cube** pieces and scale them to look like control consoles. This allows us to approximate the actual size of the 3D piece to make.

4. Using the **Shape_Pipe**, **Shape_Pipe_90**, and **Shape_Pipe_180** pieces, add some pipes around the room to add more detail. A good rule of thumb in square spaces is to add details to the corners to hide the fact that the room is square. It makes the space more interesting and provides visual variety.

5. Using the **Shape_Trim**, **Shape_Trim_90_In**, and **Shape_Trim_90_out** pieces, add some trim where the floor and walls meet. Once you finish that, select all your trim pieces, copy them, and flip them over to trim the area where the walls meet the ceiling.

6. The **Props** folder contains several completed pieces we can use, not unlike the pieces we will make using Blender later in this book. Grab a couple of chairs to add to our bridge, near our "computer console" placeholder shapes.

7. Using the **Shape_Cube** piece again, add some variety to the back and side walls.

Here is my completed whitebox of the bridge:

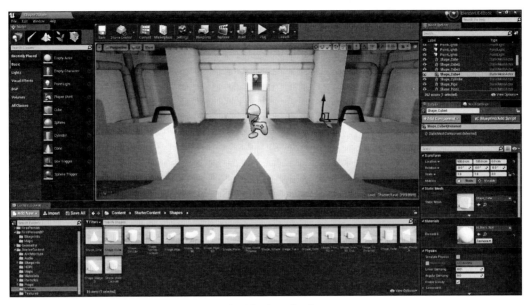

The final bridge whitebox

And my completed whitebox of the cargo bay:

The final whitebox of the cargo bay

Is it starting to feel more like an environment? If not, add a few more shapes or props until your level feels more natural. However, do not go too far. We want our level to have some objects in it to convey story and immerse the player in our environment. We don't want to overcrowd the level and have it feel clunky and cluttered. Take some time to add some detail to the hallway and the second room. In the next section, we will take a look at techniques to light our level with our theme in mind.

Using different types of light

Throughout the level, we have been using basic lights just to give our work in progress some illumination. In this section, we are going to transform our lighting into something that seems more realistic for our theme and communicates it to the player. Proper lighting is something that is important to make a scene or environment seem believable. It can make an audience feel anxious or scared, and create a sense of tension. It can communicate danger or safety. In games, it can even be a game mechanic. In our scene, we are going to use lighting to communicate a sense of mystery and a tension that something just might be going on beyond the player's ability to see.

To create this feel, let's think about what we might need. Plunging our corners into shadow and limiting the player's line of sight can go a long way to making them think that something might be stalking them, just out of sight. Using different colored lights to denote danger and safety can communicate those things to the player and thus create or relieve tension. Just like when we were gathering inspiration from online images to help with item placement, images from other games, and especially real life, can help with figuring out the right lighting for your level. Unreal provides a few different types of light to help us achieve these goals. **PointLights** are a type of light we are already familiar with. They cast light in all directions from a fixed point in space. Next we have **SpotLights**. These lights throw light in a cone shape toward a target point. This can be used to highlight specific things in an environment. Lastly, we have **DirectionalLights** and **SkyLights**. These are large light sources that create a universal amount of light throughout the level. **DirectionalLights** are often used to create the sun or moon in an outdoor environment. For each type of light, the **Details** panel provides several options for tweaking the intensity, shadows, falloff, and color. Ready to add some emotion to our environment?

1. Let's start our lighting process by deleting all but one light from each room. This will allow us to start with something very basic. Don't forget to build the level after you have made lighting changes. This allows Unreal to process the changes to the shadows and give you an accurate look at your changes.

2. Select the light located near the **PlayerStart**. The bridge area of our small ship is where the player starts and should feel at least marginally safer than the rest of the ship:

Creating a green light for the bridge

3. Change the color of the light to a pale green. This is done by selecting the light and clicking the **Light Color** option. This will bring up a color wheel that allows you to select a new color for the light.

4. At the default level, the light is too bright for our purposes. In the details panel, find the **Intensity** property and put in a lower value. I set my light to 250.

5. Lights have an area of effect that is governed by a property called **Attenuation**. This is essentially the radius in which the light goes from full power to zero. A light that has its **Attenuation** set to 0 does not have any falloff at all and is at full intensity. We want the light to not be much more than what might be put out by a computer screen. Let's set it to 250.

6. Since we wanted the light to put out only as much light as a computer screen, go ahead and move it over near our computer console shape.

7. If we look at the shadows cast by our light, they are very harsh and hard edged. Not at all what we would see in reality. Most lighting tends to create very soft and diffuse shadows and we would like to mimic that here. We do that by adding a **Source Radius** in the **Details** panel. Mine is set to `150`:

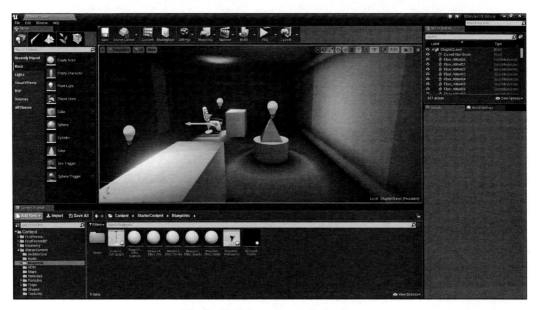

The final lighting setup on the bridge

8. Now that we have all of our settings for the light completed, let's copy the light over to our other computer console and above where our holographic display is (above the pyramid shape).

9. The following screenshot shows the final lighting setup in the cargo bay:

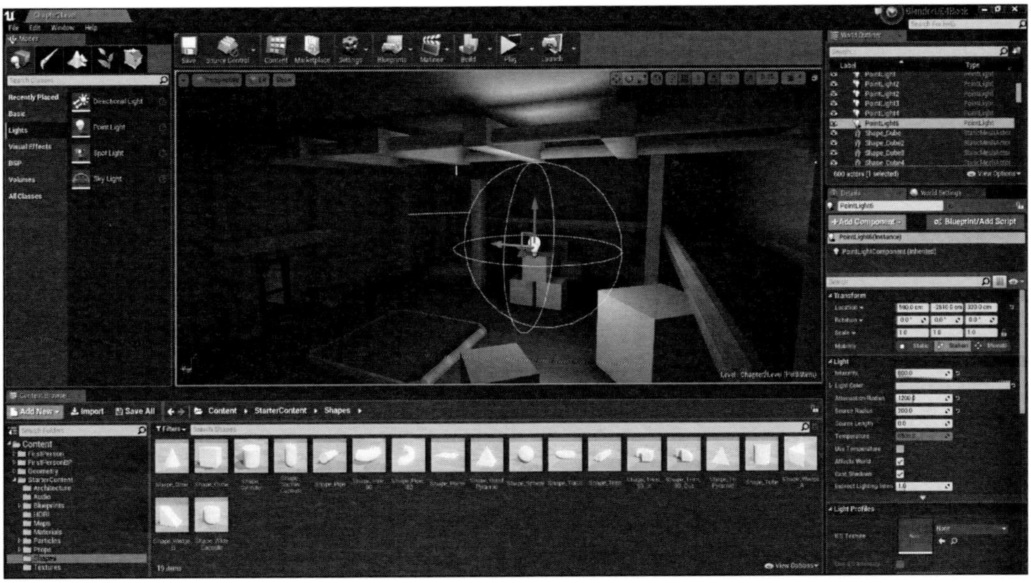

Final lighting setup for the cargo bay

Make sure to build your level and play it to check out your fully-lit bridge. Once you are happy, apply some of the same techniques we learned to the hallway and the second room, our cargo bay. Remember we are going for tension and mystery. Since these areas are outside our "safe" bridge, I like to use red and yellow light. Now let's add some fun interactive elements to our level by making the doors and elevator work.

Adding interactive elements using Triggers and Blueprints

Right now, our game level is looking pretty good. We have given it some props that make the player feel they are wandering around the insides of a small cargo ship. Using lights, we have communicated to the player a sense of danger and mystery. The final step in finishing this level will be to add some basic interactive elements. For that we are going to need a **Blueprint**.

A Blueprint is a visual scripting engine built into the Unreal game engine that allows artists and other non-programmers to program game mechanics and level events without ever looking at a line of code. I have also found during my years of teaching that it is a great way to introduce yourself to programming techniques, as a Blueprint uses many of the same terms. For our purposes, we will use Blueprints to animate our two doors and our elevator so that our player has some interactive elements to play with:

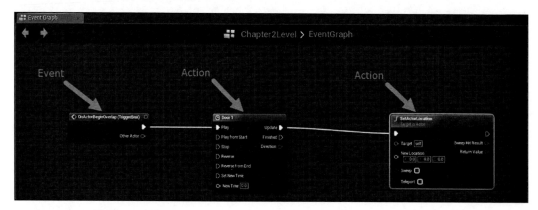

All Blueprints have an Event to kick them off, followed by one or more Actions

Most of the basic programming that we will use as a level designer follows the same basic pattern: an **Event** causes a number of **Actions** to occur. For example, to cause a door to open, the event might be that the player walks up to the door, and the actions would be to animate the door to the open position and then close it after a few seconds. As we build our Blueprint sequences, we will also learn about variables and data types. Let's get started with our door sequence:

1. First we need a **Trigger**. This is a game object that is used to detect if other objects, such as the player, have entered an area. They come in a few different shapes, and the size can be adjusted for almost any situation. Here, we will grab a **Box Trigger** from our **Modes** panel and place it at the base of our door. This will cause the event that plays our animation:

Opening up the Level Blueprint using the Blueprints menu

2. Now it's time to begin our sequence. Open the Level Blueprint by clicking on the Blueprints button and selecting **Open Level Blueprint**. Navigating the Blueprint area is done by holding the *RMB*, dragging in a direction, and using the *LMB* button to select things:

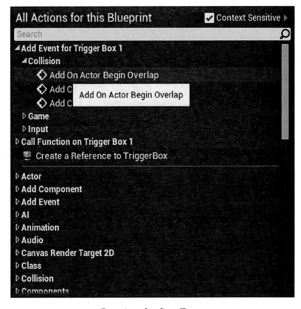

Creating the first Event

3. Go back to the level and make sure your **Trigger** is selected. Now, in the **Blueprint** window, right-click in the empty space and click the down arrow next to **Add Event** for **Trigger Box 1** (your number may be different). Click the down arrow next to **Collision** and select **Add On Actor Begin Overlap**. This event will fire when an **Actor** (our player) begins to overlap with the **Trigger**.

4. Next we need a **Timeline**. This is a node that allows you to animate a numeric datatype, such as a float or a vector. In our case, we will use it to animate the vector position of our door to make it seem like it's sliding. Right-click in the space next to your event and go down to the very bottom of the list. Select **Add Timeline**. You will be given the opportunity to give it a unique name. I named mine Door1, which is not very descriptive, but it differentiates it from any other **Timeline** we will create:

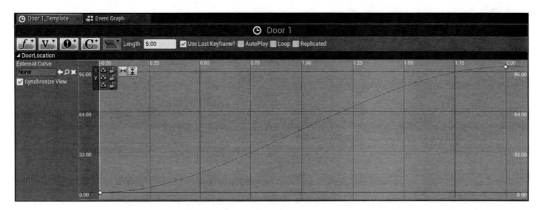

Creating the Timeline animation curve

5. Open up the **Timeline** by double-clicking on the node. Since we are animating a vector (a point in 3D space), we need to click the **V+** button located in the top left of the **Timeline** window. You will see three colored lines, which represent the **X**, **Y**, and **Z** axes. What we are going to do is create key frames that correspond to the important positions of a door: open, and closed. Before we add a keyframe though, we need to make sure we are working just in the **X** axis, since that is the direction we will be sliding our door. We do this with the little padlock beside the **Y** and **Z** in the upper left of our graph. You may also want to hide the axes by clicking the eye next to them as well.

6. Near **0**, add a key by right-clicking and selecting **Add Key** to **X** axis. If you were not exactly on zero, feel free to click the keyframe and change Time and Value to zero. Next, add another key at 2 seconds and change its value to `100`. We are telling the door to slide 100 units in the positive **X** axis direction. Lastly, we can make the sliding more realistic by right-clicking on the first key and setting **Key Interpolation** to `Auto`. You can view your handiwork by clicking the Fit Horizontal and Fit Vertical arrows (near the padlocks) to see the full curve:

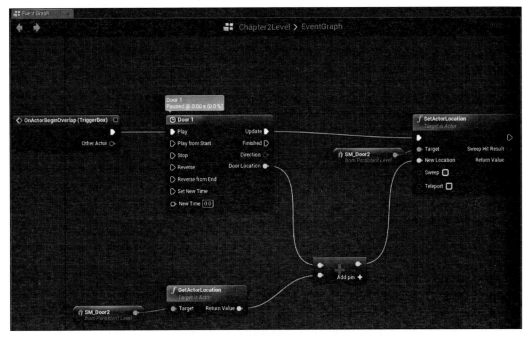

Blueprint that animates our door

7. Head back to the **Event Graph** by clicking its tab. Now we need to take advantage of our animated value by making our door move. The node we are looking for here is called **Set Actor Location**. Right-click near the **Timeline** and type this in the **Search** box. You can also use the **Find a Node** library if you have enabled your Palette in the Windows menu. **Set Actor Location** requires two pieces of information to work: the Target (what is moving) and the new location. Now, you might be tempted to connect the yellow output of our **Timeline** right to the new location, but it won't necessarily work. We need to take into account the existing location of the door and add in our slide. For that we need to get the location of our door. Click the door in the level and right-click in our Blueprint. In the search box, type in `Get Actor Location`. We also need to get a node call **Vector + Vector** to do our math for us. Connect all the nodes together, just like you see in the previous picture, by left-clicking and holding on an output (such as a colored dot or an arrow), then dragging out a "wire" and plugging into the next node's input. Don't worry too much about this part; Unreal does not allow you to plug a node into another node that doesn't accept that input.

8. Now, our Get and Set nodes are still missing something. Neither node has a target, so they don't know which object to reference. For that, we need a **Name** variable. This is just a reference to something present in the level. In the level, click on the door we want to animate. Now in the Blueprint, right-click next to our **Set Actor Location** node and select **Create a Reference** to **SM_Door2** (again, your number may be different). Now, plug that variable into the target of our node. Repeat this process to create a name variable for our **Get Actor Location** node.

9. The last part of the process is to go back into the level, click on the door, and select **Movable** in the **Transform** section of the **Details** panel. This will allow your door to animate. Now build the level and test it out.

10. Everything working? Great! Make sure to follow the process again for the second door at the other end of the hallway.

Now that we have moving doors, we are going to do the same thing to our elevator, only this time we will use a slightly different process. **Matinee** is a powerful tool that allows animators and game designers to create high quality animations inside Unreal. We are going to use this tool to animate our elevator:

1. Creating a **Matinee** is a bit different from creating a **Timeline**. To start a Matinee, click on the **Matinee** button and select **Add Matinee**. Unreal will give you a warning that **Undo/Redo** data will reset. Go ahead and click **Continue** and this will create a Matinee object in your level. Don't worry about its location, this thing works from anywhere. Click on the object and select **Open Matinee** over in the **Details** panel. The following screenshot shows the **Matinee** tool:

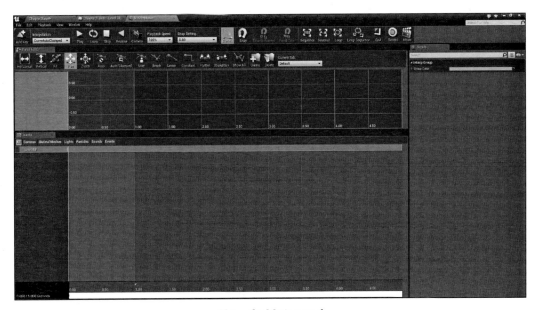

Using the Matinee tool

2. Back in the level, click on our elevator platform and make sure it is set to **Movable** in the **Details** panel. Now click back in the **Matinee**. In the **Tracks** section of the matinee screen, we are going to right-click and select **Create New Empty Group** from the menu. Name it something unique, such as `Elevator`. This creates a group for any objects we want to animate regarding the elevator.

3. Next, right-click on the group you just created and select **Create New Movement Track**. This will create the actual animation track in which we can add our keyframes:

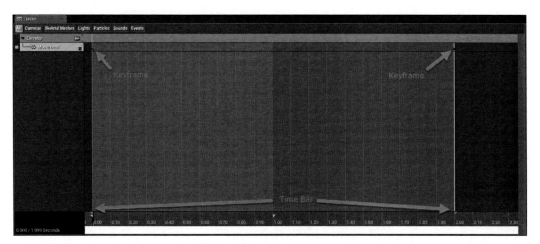

The Matinee interface

4. When you created the **Movement** track, Unreal created your first keyframe at **0**. This will be our down position. To create a second key for our up position, click the **Add Key** button located in the top left of the **Matinee** screen. Right-click that key and select **Set Time**. Input 2 in the box and press *Enter*. With our second key still selected, go to the level and move our elevator into the up position. We will know that it worked when we see a dotted line created that goes from our down position to our new up position. Lastly, change the length of the total **Matinee** sequence by grabbing the red tab at the bottom of the Time Bar near **5** and dragging it down to **2**. With that done, let's close our **Matinee**:

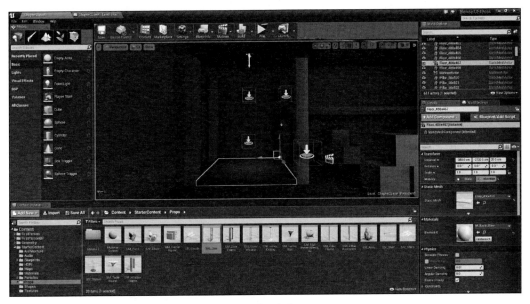

The completed elevator

5. At this point, we need some buttons in our level to control our elevator. Go ahead and head over to the **Shapes** folder, like we have done in the past, and grab a couple of shapes we can use as call buttons. I used a pyramid that had been scaled down a bit to fit on the pillars and walls near the platform. We also need to add **Box Triggers** around each of our buttons to create an activation area the player needs to be in to use the button:

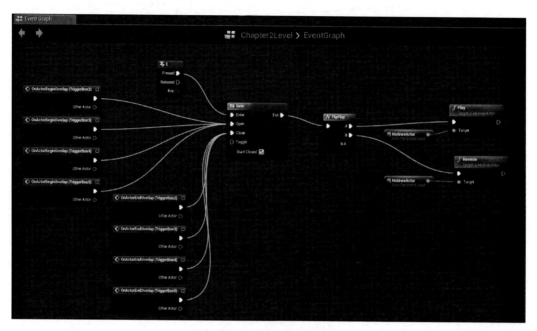

The blueprint for the elevator

6. With all of our buttons and **Box Triggers** in place, it's time to assemble the **Blueprint** sequence. In the level, select all of your Box Triggers we will be using. In the Blueprint window, right-click and select **Add Event for Selected Actors**. This will allow you to create an **On Actor Begin Overlap** and an **On Actor End Overlap** for all the Trigger Boxes at the same time. We also need to search for an input event for pressing *E*.

7. The next node we need is a **Gate**. These nodes allow you to control the flow of information through the sequence. Information enters the gate through the **Enter** input and only continues if the **Gate** is open. In our elevator control (see the preceding picture), pressing *E* will send information into the **Gate**, but the gate will only be open if the player is standing next to one of the elevator control buttons.

8. After the **Gate** node, we need the aptly named **Flip Flop** node. This node will execute either A or B, depending on which branch was last executed. This will allow us to toggle the elevator up and down by playing and reversing our **Matinee**.

9. Now we want to tell our sequence to **Play** and **Reverse** the Matinee. Click on the **Matinee** object back in our level. Come back into the Blueprint and right click, then select to create a reference to our **Matinee Actor**. Drag a wire off the Matinee Actor and search for the **Play** and **Reverse** nodes. Add these to the Blueprint.

10. Now wire the Blueprint like you see in the image, click the **Compile** button, and give the level a test!

Learning to read the programming logic of Blueprints can be a huge help when we begin to create things that have never been done before. For our elevator Blueprint, we can talk it through by starting with the Event and going through each action. For example, our elevator starts by pressing *E*. The gate checks to see if the player is near a button or not. If it is, the elevator Matinee will either Play or Reverse, depending on what it did last. Learning from existing Blueprint sequences is great practice!

Playtesting our level

The next step in our design process is to playtest our prototype level with friends, family, and, most importantly, the people who will be playing our game. Playtesting is one of the most important and overlooked steps of the design process. Many game and level designers want to rush and press on toward a final design and, by doing so, miss out on the valuable feedback that other people who are not involved with the design and construction of your game can offer. It is important to remember that although the level may be fun for you to play, others may find it confusing or missing critical features. Getting feedback from players by allowing them to try the prototype can help us see the things that we take for granted because we are the designers.

If this level were for a commercial game, we would spend some time testing with friends and co-workers, incorporating feedback as we go. The lighting might be too dark or the buttons too difficult to find. We might add more rooms or a puzzle to make the level more of a challenge. We could even scrap the whole thing and start over if we were receiving consistent feedback that people didn't understand the reason it was there. The important thing to remember with playtesting is that your players' feedback is not a criticism of you or your idea. The information you gather from them is meant to improve your levels and strengthen your designs, so never miss an opportunity to gather this important data!

Summary

In this chapter, we went through the process of building a level using Unreal Engine 4, based on a design we sketched out on paper. The level itself was simple: two rooms connected by a hallway with doors, stairs, and an elevator. We used a selection of shapes and props that were available in the `Starter Content` folder to decorate our space to fit our science fiction horror theme. We also looked at how to use lights in the level to create tension and convey mood. Through Blueprints, we were able to explore level programming by animating our doors and elevator. Finally, we talked about the importance of playtesting and how constructive criticism from our players can only make our levels and games better. In the next chapter, we are going to move into using Blender and create a prop for our level, based on some of the basic shapes we used to decorate the ship during the whiteboxing process.

3
It's Time to Customize!

How did your level turn out?

Does it feel like a cargo ship?

How did your play testers feel while playing it?

Remember that one of the purposes of whiteboxing a level is to get an idea for the props that we need and their relative sizes. If we were going to take this level all the way through development (and feel free to finish the level after this chapter), we would replace every basic shape with a detailed custom game asset. However, that is a bit outside the scope of this book. What we will do is build a basic prop to get you started with **Blender** and get you comfortable with the process of bringing custom art into Unreal. With some practice, the only limit to your level building ability will be your imagination! In this chapter, we will cover the following topics:

- Getting started making game assets
- Using the basic tools of polygon modeling
- How to use UV mapping and why it's important
- UV unwrapping our game asset
- Basic texturing techniques

Getting started making game assets

So, before we get started designing our asset, which asset will we be building? During our whiteboxing, we used several basic shapes to represent potential game assets and this gives us many to choose from, such as a hologram projector, computer console, pipes, columns, or crates. Since this is likely to be your first foray into using Blender, we will start by creating a detailed crate for our cargo ship to be transporting. A crate allows us to build something that is fairly basic but can still support a lot of detail. So go ahead and grab yourself another piece of graph paper and open your web browser; it's time to sketch!

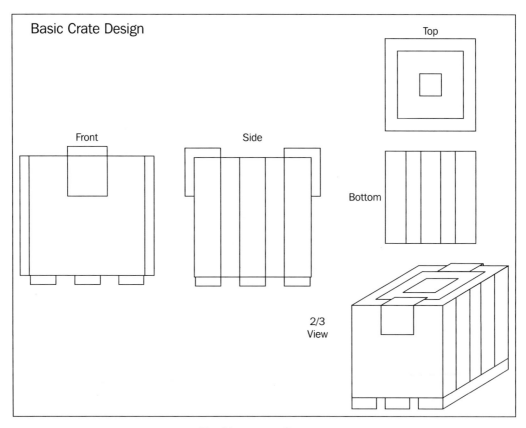

Sketching out our first asset

My design is based on bits and pieces of several different sci-fi crates I found online and that I remembered from some of my favorite games and movies (sci-fi happens to be one of my favorite genres). The crate itself is also designed to have an inside, so I can show it in my level with both the lid on and off. This gives the asset flexibility and allows me to use it in many different situations, two very important design considerations.

Reuse of assets is important to game design and development due to the large amount of work it takes to build unique environments. Many building sets available in the Unreal Marketplace are designed to be modular to create a variety of different scenes. This practice goes back to even the earliest game titles. In Super Mario Bros. on the NES, the clouds and bushes are the exact same game asset, just different colors.

You may have noticed that I did a few different views of my crate. This allows us to see our object from the front, side, and back, and design an object with some variety to each section. By doing this, we can also communicate the design to another artist on the team if we're the ones who created the design but not the ones who will be building the asset in 3D.

Now let's set up our file in Blender (remember our settings from *Chapter 1, Unreal, My Friend, I'd Like You to Meet Blender*?):

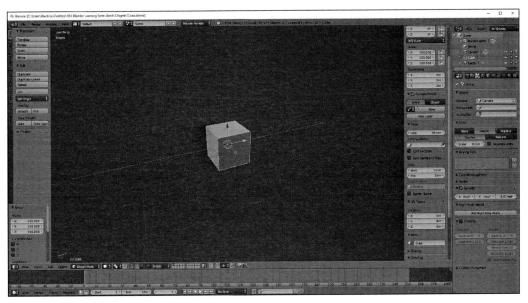

Setting our scale to match Unreal 4

1. Open **Blender**.
2. Change the unit scale to **Metric** in the **Scene** portion of the **Properties** pane.

3. Change the **Scale** to `0.01`.

4. Press *N* to open the **Scene Properties** pane and fix the grid by changing the **Clip End** property under **View** to `1.0 km`.

5. Scale your starter cube by `100` since we will be using it.

6. Click the **File** menu and select **Save Startup File**. This will save our changes as the default settings and make sure that all the files we create going forward will have these settings. This will save us time in the future.

With our Blender file ready to go, it's time to begin building our crate.

Using the basic tools of polygon modeling

We will begin building our crate with the primitive object that is closest to the finished shape we want. In this case, the default cube we start with works great. So what is a primitive and why do we start with one? Primitive shapes are your basic shapes, in the case of Blender: plane, cube, circle, sphere, cylinder, cone, and torus. We start with these shapes since they are the basic building blocks of all we see. Traditional artists start with these when they draw as well. If you take a look outside, you can see these shapes: poles are cylinders, buildings are cubes, and so on. That is also the reason why Unreal gives us a Shapes folder full of primitives to block out our levels with.

One of the easiest 3D modeling techniques to learn is Polygon modeling, or simply, poly modeling. It involves manipulating the vertices, edges, and polygons that make up a primitive shape to create something greater. Poly modeling uses the following tools:

The Tools panel

Extrude: This tool allows you to push a polygon in or pull it out and is very useful in creating new portions of an object:

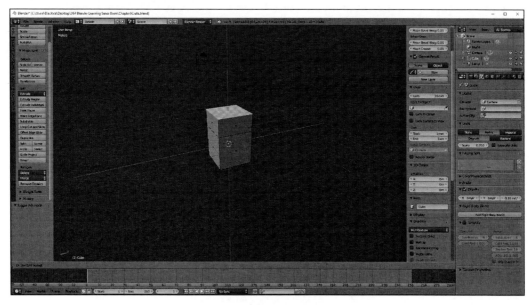

Using the Extrude tool

Inset Faces: Inset is useful for creating details within an object, such as creating windows or doors on a building:

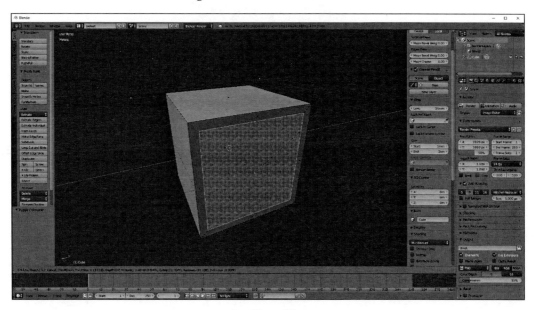

Insetting a face

Loop Cut and Slide: Another tool for adding detail, it cuts new edge loops into your object. The number of edge loops to be added can be adjusted by using the mouse wheel:

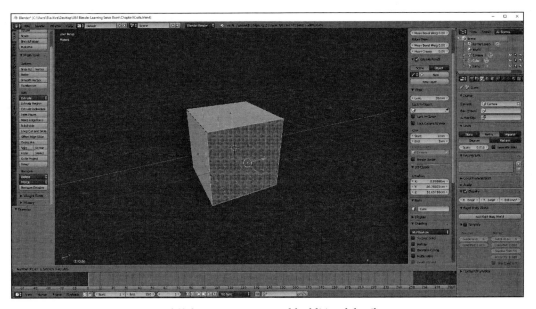

Loop Cut and Slide is a great way to add additional detail to an asset

The other tools in the palette are situational, but there is one more I would like to talk about that is not in this menu.

Bevel: Found in the specials menu (press *W*), the **Bevel** tool allows you to round an edge off. The number of additional edges to add can be adjusted by using the mouse wheel:

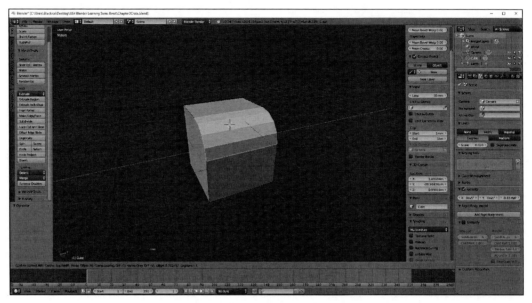

Bevel can create a rounded corner with ease

Time to start transforming our cube into something worthy of our level. The first thing we need to do is get the basic shape of our crate down:

1. Select the cube and press the *Tab* key. This will switch you from **Object** mode to **Edit** mode. **Object** mode is used for adding new objects to your scene and arranging those objects using the move, rotate, and scale tools. **Edit** mode allows you to manipulate the vertices, edges, and polygons of the object you had selected when you switched modes:

The selection mode buttons

2. Switch to polygon selection. The selection mode buttons can be found along the bottom of the 3D window:

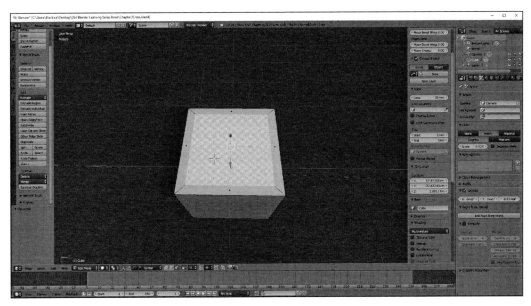

Insetting the face that will be the top of our crate

3. Select the top poly and press *I* to use the **Inset** tool. Inset the polygon to create the frame shape, like we have in our sketch. You can also type in a value (I used 0.177) and press *Enter*.

4. Press *E* to use the **Extrude** tool. Push the polygon in to give the crate top a good edge.

5. We are going to **Inset** again. Inset the polygon again to create the space for our control box. I used `0.523` as my value. Now extrude the small polygon up to create the control box:

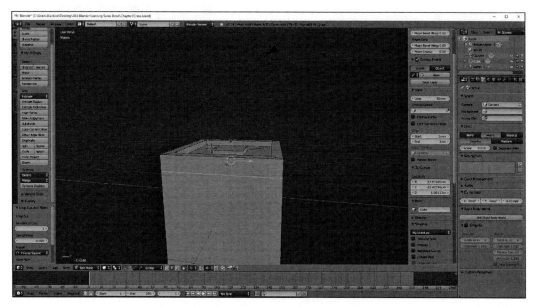

Creating more detail with Loop Cut and Slide

6. Now we need to cut the line to create the seam where the top fits on to the crate. Click the **Loop Cut and Slide** tool from the menu on the left or press *Ctrl+R*. Move the mouse over the crate until you have one purple line cutting horizontally across the lower section. Click *LMB*, this will turn the line orange and allow you to slide it up and down along the crate. Click again when it is in the location we want.

7. Split this new line with the **Bevel** tool. Press *W* and select **Bevel**. I split mine by `0.05`:

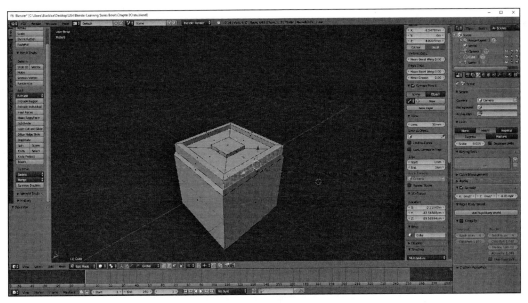

Creating our lid seam using the Scale tool

8. One more step for the lid: select the four polygons around the outside of the lid (hold the *Shift* key to select multiple polygons) and scale them down a little by pressing *S* to use the **Scale** tool.

9. Next we will add the detailing along the sides. Along the *Y* axis (the green axis), we are going to use the **Loop Cut and Slide** tool and cut four lines vertically around our object.

10. Move the mouse to get the purple guidelines going vertically along our crate and then use the mouse wheel until we have four lines. Click the mouse to cut the lines and then click it again without moving the mouse to keep them centered:

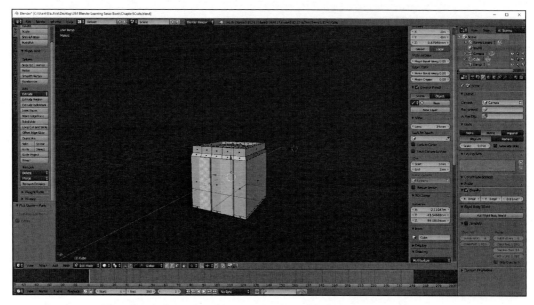

Extruding polygons to add some raised areas to the crate along the sides

11. Now we are going to select a few of our new polygons to create the bands along the sides of our box. **Extrude** those using the **Extrude Individual** tool and pull them out to a good size. Also **Extrude** the runners for the bottom of the box by pulling out the two outside polygons and the middle polygon:

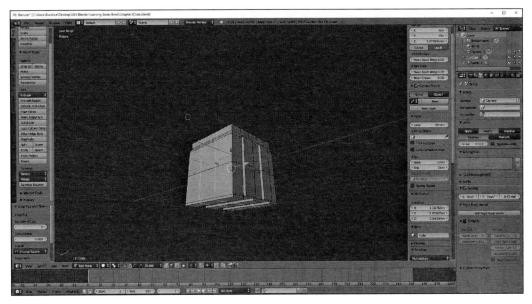

Creating the latch

12. Let's add the latch. Add a horizontal edge loop around our crate using **Loop Cut and Slide**. Then add two vertical edge loops to the front of the crate:

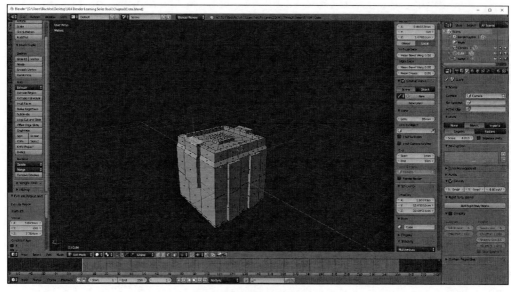

Finishing the latch

13. Finishing the latch is a two-step **Extrude** process. Select the three polygons shown and **Extrude** them out. Then select the two on the top of the latch and **Extrude** those:

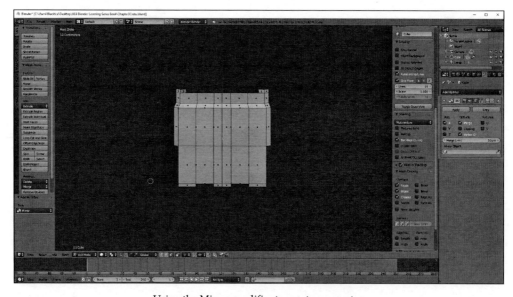

Using the Mirror modifier to create symmetry

14. Now to make sure everything is even, we will use a **Mirror** modifier. Cut our object in half by using **Loop Cut and Slide** to cut a vertical line from front to back. Next, press *B* to do a window selection and select half of the crate. Press the *Delete* key and select **Faces** to delete half of the crate.

15. Lastly, add the **Mirror** modifier by clicking the wrench icon in the **Properties** pane to open up the **Modifier** menu. Click the **Add Modifier** dropdown and select **Mirror**. Manipulate the settings until you have successfully made our object whole again. Once everything is set, go back to **Object** mode and click **Apply** in the **Modifier** menu. Modifiers cannot be added in **Edit** mode. Finished! Not bad for our first prop. It looks like it could fit just about anything, from food to horribly mutated genetic monsters that hunt you in the dark.

How to use UV mapping and why it's important

At this point, we have the geometry, or basic shape of our crate down, but it still doesn't really look like the objects we see in other games. The reason is textures. Texturing our object will create all those little details that will make our game asset worthy of the level we have built. Making our textures and getting them on the object is a two-step process. First, we need to tell our textures how to behave and that takes a UV map:

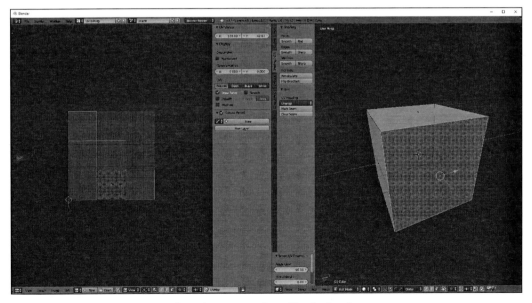

Learning unwrapping with a basic cube

A UV map is a set of coordinates that tell texture maps we have placed on a game asset how to wrap themselves around our object. The principle is to take your 3D object and flatten it, so that we can apply an image to the outside in a manner that doesn't tear or stretch the texture. This allows us to create detailed texture maps that apply things like scraped edges, rust spots, paint colors, visual screens, and more. Without it, Unreal will not know how to texture our object in game. It will also not be able to apply lighting correctly, since Unreal uses UV maps to apply light and shadow:

The UV mapping menu

So how do we do this in Blender? The application gives us several options for adding a UV map, some of which are more useful for what we have created than others:

- **Smart UV Project**: Useful for architectural and mechanical objects, Smart UV Project creates a custom UV layout based on angular changes to your geometry. It does its best to lay everything out in a logical fashion and can minimize stretching. The tool tries to lay things logically but may need a bit of tweaking.

- **Cube Projection**: Cube mapping breaks your object into six faces and projects them on to planes. This creates six separate UV islands that can be manipulated.

- **Project From View**: Creates a UV map based on what is selected and the angle of the 3D view. For example, you can select all of the polygons on the left-hand side of the object and select the **Left Side** view for the viewport and use this option.

- **Lightmap Pack**: Unreal and other game engines use a lightmap to bake shadows on to objects during building. Lightmap Pack can create a UV layout that is more suited to lightmaps by using as much UV space as possible. This maximizes the amount of lighting information the object can take and will improve the results.

UV unwrapping our game asset

UV mapping can be a difficult process, but understanding some best practices can help make the process easier:

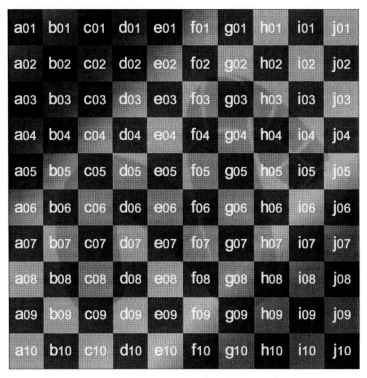

A UV grid texture map

1. Use a colored UV grid texture during the process: This can be easily found using an online image search, and can be applied to your object in Blender as a material. Be sure to find one the same size as the texture you wish to create, such as 1024 x 1024 or 2048 x 2048. I used a 2048 x 2048 image.

2. Minimize seams and stretching: It is important to hide the seams of your UV map along hard edges or in hidden areas not seen by the player. Luckily for us, hard surface objects such as our crate are easier to unwrap than objects with more organic curves such as cars, plants, or animals.

3. Be consistent with the orientation of your UV elements: When laying out your UV map, keeping everything oriented in the same direction will make laying out and creating your texture map that much easier. This is even more important if the texture artist is another member on the team.

4. Be careful not to waste space: Less wasted space in your texture map translates directly to increased pixel density in your texture and better quality overall.

5. Remember that all these things take practice to master.

Now let's UV unwrap our crate:

Changing the viewports to the UV Editing preset using the Scene Layout dropdown

1. Select our crate and enter **Edit** mode, if you are not already there. Also make sure you are in polygon selection mode. Press *A* twice to select all the polygons of the crate.

2. In the Menu Bar, go to the **Scene Layout** dropdown and select **UV Editing**. This will split the viewport into two halves. The left side is your UV layout and will be blank for the time being. The right half is your object. You can still move and rotate it so you can grab different polygons.

3. In the 3D viewport (right side), you will notice that the Tools panel has changed to the **Shading/UV** tools. Under the **UVs** heading there is the **UV Mapping** option drop-down menu. These options are where we begin UV unwrapping an object. With all of the polygons selected, open the menu and select the **Smart UV Project** option:

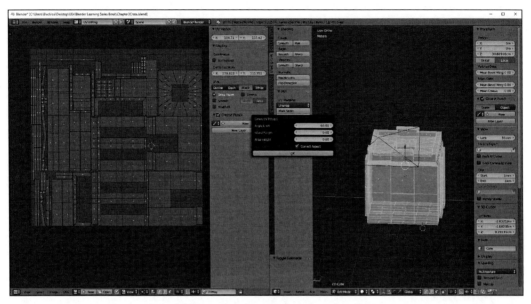

A basic UV layout using Smart UV Project

4. **Smart UV Project** is Blender's auto unwrap tool. Most 3D creation suites have one and their output can vary depending on how complicated your object is. For a simple crate like ours we will get fairly good results. For something more organic or for machines or architecture that are complicated, it might be hard to get a good result. At the Smart UV Project menu, we are going to use the default settings. Click **Ok** and it will unwrap your object.

5. **Smart UV Project** has mashed our object flat and flat and separated it into UV islands. A UV island is a piece of your object. For our purposes, the way Blender has separated out our object will work just fine. If we were making a more complicated object, we could separate out each piece, group them to make more sense, and even stitch some of the pieces back together. This step will be necessary later in the book, when we create a more complicated object.

6. To improve the quality of our map, we can use the **Pack Islands** option found in the UVs menu at the bottom of the UV Layout viewport. Selecting this option will resize all of your UV islands to take up as much space as possible without causing stretching.

7. Since we are working in a game engine, we will need a second UV channel, or set of coordinates, for lighting information. To add another UV channel, we need to head back to the **Scene Layout** dropdown and select **Default**:

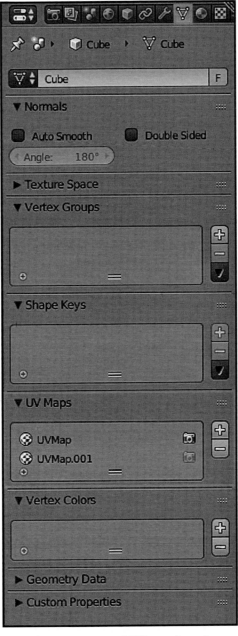

Creating our second UV map channel

In the **Properties** panel, click on the icon for **Object Data**. Under the **UV Maps** heading, click the plus button to create another UV channel.

8. On this second UV channel, we are going to add our lightmap UVs. These differ from our UV layout for texturing in that we don't care about making sure all the pieces are scaled to the same value. We only care that they take up as much space as possible to store light and shadow info. Blender's **Lightmap Pack** tool can easily do that for us. Head back to the **UV Layout** option in the **Scene Layout** drop-down menu. In the lower-right corner of the UV Layout viewport is the active UV channel. It will say **UVMap**. Click it and select **UVMap.001**. This is our new channel:

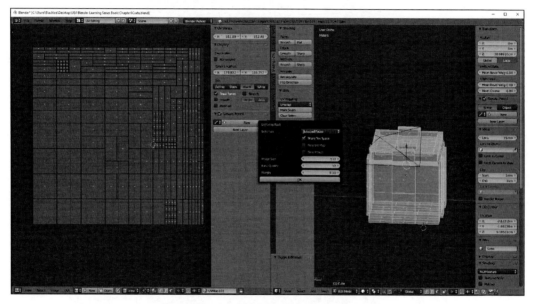

Using the Lightmap Pack tool to create a lightmap that Unreal 4 can use

9. Head over to the **Tools** panel on the 3D viewport side and select **Lightmap Pack** from the **UV Mapping** menu. The default options are OK here as well. Click **Ok**. Now that we are done unwrapping. Head back to the **Default** screen layout:

Adding the UV texture grid as a texture map to our crate

10. To test our UV layout, we can add the colored UV texture grid we downloaded earlier. This will easily show us if there is any stretching of our texture. If we were unwrapping this by hand, this texture map would help us put together a UV map and ensure all of our elements are facing one direction and minimize stretching. Click on the **Textures** button on the **Properties** panel toolbar. In the first section of the menu, go to the **Type** dropdown and select **Image or Movie**. This will open up the **Image** section of the menu and allow you to click the **Open** button. Navigate to where you stored your image and select it.

11. Click the icon in the **Properties** panel toolbar next to the **Texture** icon. This is the **Materials** panel. All that is left to do is to **Assign** the material to your object. Click the **Select** option to select all your polygons, then click **Assign**. This adds the material to our object. It is stretched around the object according to our UV map.

12. Obviously, we don't want a super colorful box in our Unreal environment. In the next section we will talk about adding our own basic material to the box and about other techniques for creating detailed textures.

Basic texturing techniques

As I mentioned earlier, textures are what make a game object pop in your level. They can be used to add all kinds of different elements we would not take the time to model, as well as color, wear and tear, and lighting information. There are many ways to texture our game object. Basic objects that would like to take advantage of a material in Unreal can apply one in the level. Blender has painting tools available within the program through its texture paint mode. Lastly, there are options available using other programs to create your textures. Our UV map can be exported to a program like **Adobe Photoshop** or **GIMP**, where we can paint the textures using the color tools or use photos to create a realistic result. I also want to talk about a new type of tool that has been available for a couple of years now. **Substance Painter** is an application that allows you to paint textures directly on to your 3D object, much like Blender's texture painting mode, but it has options and tools built specifically for the digital entertainment industry:

Showing off our new crate within Unreal 4

Unreal comes with several materials available for our use through the `Starter Content` folder and since our UV map is going to import in with our object, it would be as simple as dragging and dropping the material on to our crate. The materials themselves would look great on the crate and would definitely provide the depth and character we would want for our level. However, since the materials are not made specifically for our crate they would not really provide some of the additional detail that we talked about earlier. When we import our object into Unreal in our next chapter, we will first try this route:

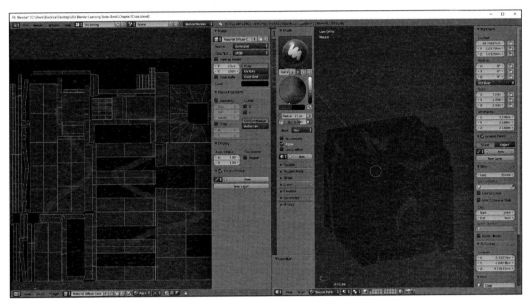

Blender's Texture Paint mode

Blender itself comes with a Texture Paint mode. This mode can be used to paint solid colors and images on to an object. The resulting texture can then be exported from the program and applied within Unreal. Using this mode allows us to create our texture for our crate without involving any other programs, but since Blender is not a dedicated graphics editing program, the tools it provides are limited:

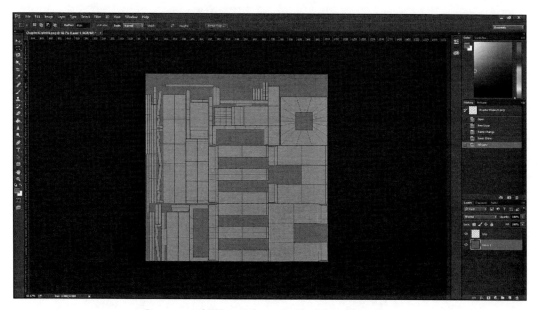

Our exported UV map shown inside Adobe Photoshop

Adobe Photoshop, and its open source alternative GIMP, are graphics editing programs that can be used for many forms of digital drawing, photo editing, and more. By importing our UV map into one of these programs, we can use their drawing tools to create detailed textures that can be imported into Unreal along with our object. This has been the most common way of creating game textures for many years. Adobe Photoshop is available for a 30-day trial subscription at `http://www.adobe.com/products/photoshop.html`. GIMP can be downloaded at `http://www.gimp.org`:

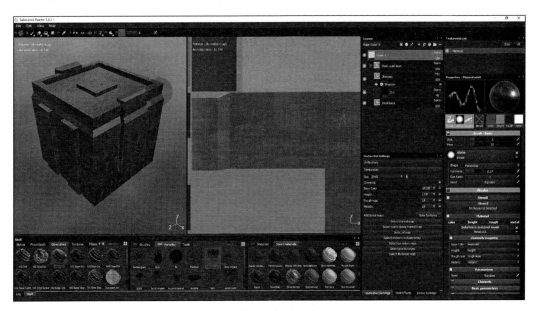

Our crate inside Allegorithmic Substance Painter

Allegorithmic Substance Painter, and other programs like it such as the **Quixel** suite of tools, is a 3D painting program that allows you to paint advanced materials directly on to your object in real time. It has many of the tools you see in Adobe Photoshop or GIMP, such as the ability to mask off areas and use different patterned brushes, but has adapted them fully to the needs of 3D game artists. Substance Painter currently has full support in the Unreal game engine and is a great way to create high-end, detailed materials in a relatively short amount of time. Check out Substance Painter at `https://www.allegorithmic.com/products/substance-painter`.

Summary

In *Chapter 3, It's Time to Customize!*, we went through using our design process to design a crate that is perfect for our cargo ship level. After designing our game asset on paper, we opened up Blender to create our 3D model using polygon modeling techniques. Within Blender, we used such tools as Extrude, Inset, Loop Cut and Slide, and Bevel, to turn a basic primitive shape into a detailed game asset. After we finished the basic geometry of our crate, we opened up the UV mapping portion of Blender and created a UV map. The UV map will handle getting both the textures we will add to the object in the next chapter, and lighting information to make sure the object blends in nicely with our level lighting. Lastly, we talked about some different ways to apply materials to our object, from simply applying a premade material to it in Unreal, to painting the object in Blender, to drawing detailed textures in Photoshop or GIMP. We also looked at the future of next-gen texturing with Substance Painter. In the next chapter, we will be exporting our object out of Blender and bringing it into Unreal so that we can use it in our level.

4
Getting the Assets to the Level

In the last chapter, we used our whitebox level to determine which of our simple shapes would be the first to be turned into a 3D asset. Having settled on turning the cubes in our cargo hold into crates, we used Blender to create our 3D game asset and UV unwrap it for use in Unreal. But how do we get it from Blender to Unreal? For that, we have to go through the process of exporting our object from Blender as an FBX file and importing it into Unreal. Then we can connect the newly imported static mesh to a material, add collision primitives, and add it into our level as a usable object. This process is called the **art pipeline**. In this chapter, we will cover the following topics:

- Exporting our object from Blender
- What is FBX?
- Importing our object into Unreal
- Setting up and using our new 3D game asset

Exporting our object from Blender

We dreamed up our creation.

We sketched our crate.

We modeled and UV unwrapped it in Blender.

Unreal is now ready to receive our creation.

Before we export our model from Blender, there are a few things we can do to make sure everything comes out perfect. Unreal can get finicky when it comes to importing objects, and with just a few steps we can minimize any potential issues.

Let's get started by applying scaling:

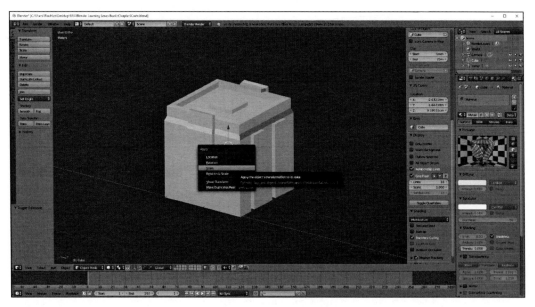

Applying scaling to our object

During the process of setting up our scene, we scaled the default cube so we could use it as a starting point when building our crate. To ensure we do not have any problems during the exporting process, we need to apply our scaling to the object; this essentially tells Blender that the object is no longer scaled but is really that size:

1. Make sure you are in **Object** mode.
2. Press *Ctrl + A*, this will open the **Apply** menu.
3. Select **Scale**.

With our scaling applied, we can move on the next important step in prepping our object for export, setting our pivot point:

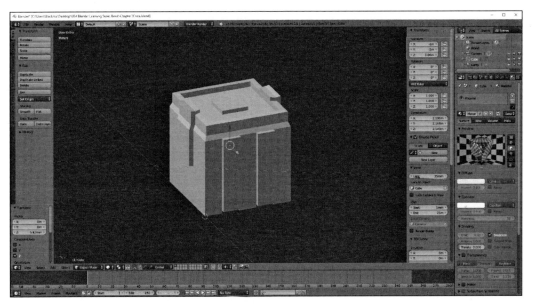

Setting the pivot point by moving our object so that the origin is at the corner of our crate

When an object is used in Unreal, it has a pivot point which acts as an anchor to the grid and as a point of reference for scaling and rotation. When creating game assets, we want to give some thought to how they will be used. For example, walls need to line up with their neighbors, so we would make sure that their measurements were even and that the pivot point was set to a corner. For something like a light fixture, we might place the pivot point so that the object would sit flat against the wall for easy placement. For our crate, we need to be able to line up the object so that it is flush with the floor. For that reason we need to move the pivot to a corner of the object that sits on the ground.

So how does Unreal decide where the pivot point of the object should be? When an object is imported into Unreal, the software takes a look at where the world origin is (**0, 0, 0** in your modeling software's grid system) and places the pivot point there. In Blender, that point is set to the center of your starting cube by default. We want to change where that pivot point is placed so that it is on the floor and in the corner of our object:

1. Press *N* to open the **Scene Properties** pane if it is not already open.

2. Raise our crate so that it is sitting on top of the grid plane. You can be exact by finding **Location:** in the **Transform** section of the **Scene Properties** pane. There you can see the **X**, **Y**, and **Z** axes of our object is set to **0, 0, 0**. Change the **Z** value so that the runners on the underside of our crate are flush with the grid plane. Mine is set at `1.06m`.

3. Change the **X** value to `-1m`.

4. Change the **Y** value to `-1m`.

All set! The pivot point will be set as the lower corner for our crate. There is one more thing we have to do with our crate in Blender before we move to exporting and that is to decide what part of our crate is the front:

Rotating the crate so that Unreal recognizes the front of the crate as the front

Unreal determines what the front of an object is by checking to see which portion of the object is facing in the positive *X*-axis direction. This is less important for our crate, but can be very important for other game assets such as characters, vehicles, and weapons.

By completing this step in Blender, we can save ourselves a lot of time rotating our objects in Unreal after being exported:

1. Referring back to our sketch of the crate, the sides had the two large latches, so our object needs to be rotated.
2. Press *R* or select rotate from the **Tools** pane.
3. Press *Z* to lock the rotation around the Z-axis.
4. Type in 90 and press *Enter*.

We are all set. We should not have any problems bringing our object into Unreal. Time to export our object out of Blender. This is done with the **FBX Exporter**.

What is FBX?

So what is the FBX file format anyway? (I know, a question you have always asked yourself.) FBX is a file extension created by a company called Kaydara for their animation program Filmbox in 1996. Kaydara was later acquired by Autodesk and the application was renamed MotionBuilder. Under the software developer Autodesk, the format has become one of the most popular formats for game assets for a number of reasons. First, it does a great job of exporting geometry and is supported by many of the most popular 3D applications. Second, it is capable of exporting your materials settings. When you import FBX files into Unreal for example, you have the option of bringing texture and material information with you, which can save time. Lastly, it is capable of exporting animation information. This will be important later, in *Chapter 8, Lights, Camera, Animation!*, when we create an animated asset for our level.

One of the only downsides to FBX is that it is a proprietary file format. Autodesk makes it available to the public through many of their products and through a software development kit. From that, members of the Blender community have been able to create an exporting tool that allows us to use this versatile file format in our projects. Let's take a look at the FBX exporter.

Importing our object into Unreal

Time to export our crate from Blender:

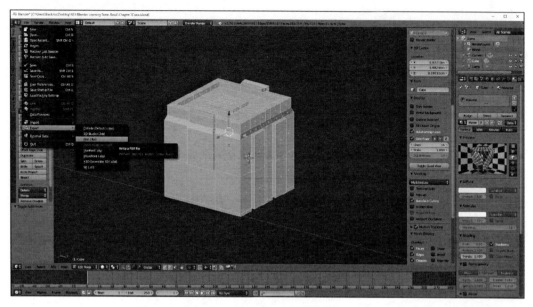

Selecting export from the File menu

The export options can be found by going to the **File** menu, then **Export**, and selecting **FBX** as your chosen file format:

FBX exporting options menu. Select the Mesh tab.

The exporter has many options, several of which we will use later as they pertain to animation. We will need to change some of the options to export our crate:

1. In the main menu of the exporter, select **Mesh**. This way, the only object that will be exported is our crate and not the camera or light that is also in the scene:

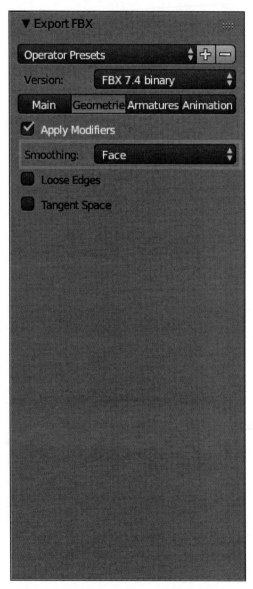

Setting our Smoothing option to Face in the Geometries tab

2. In the **Geometry** menu, change the **Smoothing** option to **Face**. Unreal requires that smoothing groups be part of any exported object even though we haven't really used them to create our crate. By selecting this option, we avoid any error messages when we import our FBX file.

3. Once you have changed those settings, save your FBX in a place where you can find it.

Next, we will open Unreal and import the file into our level. Once we hook up a few options the crate will be ready to use.

Setting up and using our new 3D asset

Now that we have our FBX file, we need to import the file into the **Content Browser** in Unreal. Epic Games has made this a relatively painless process. After we import the file into the game engine, it still needs two more things. A collision mesh will have to be added to make sure that the player and other game object collide correctly with our new crate. Second, we will have to add a material to our object to give it visual appeal.

Start by navigating in the **Content Browser** to the folder you would like to store your crate in and clicking the **Import** button:

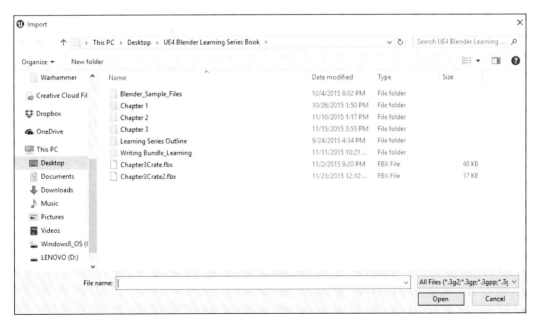

Find your FBX file in the file browser.

1. Navigate to the folder where you saved your FBX file and click **Open**:

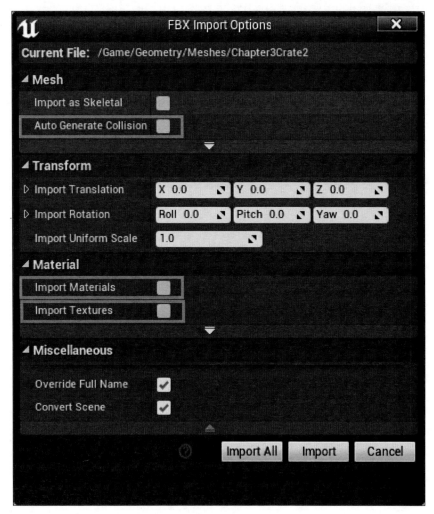

Unreal's FBX Import Options menu

2. This opens the **FBX Import Options**. Turn off the **Auto Generate Collision** option. Though this can save us time in the future, we will create this manually after we have successfully imported the file.

3. Also turn off the **Import Materials** and **Import Textures** options. These can be used if you have created a material in your 3D package and want to bring it in along with your object. If we were to use it in this case, Unreal would import our colored UV grid.

4. Once you have changed these options, click the **Import** button.

A light blue icon showing our crate should be added to the Browser. Double clicking it will take us to the **Static Mesh** editor. Here, we can set several different options that will affect every copy of the crate we use in the level:

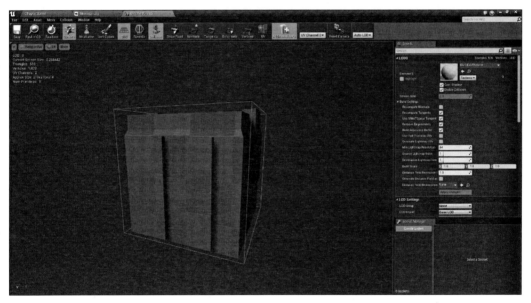

Static Mesh Editor within Unreal 4

We will start by adding a collision primitive. **Collisions** are really what make video game worlds go round and it is the way that the computer knows if a player has successfully interacted with another game object. As players, we often see collision when we stand on a platform and look down. It often looks as if we are floating just above the actual object we are standing on. This is due to the fact that the game programming actually ignores the art that the player sees and only uses the simple collision primitives that are invisible to the player to record hits. As far as we are concerned as level builders, a collision will keep the player from walking through our crate and make it so they can actually interact with it:

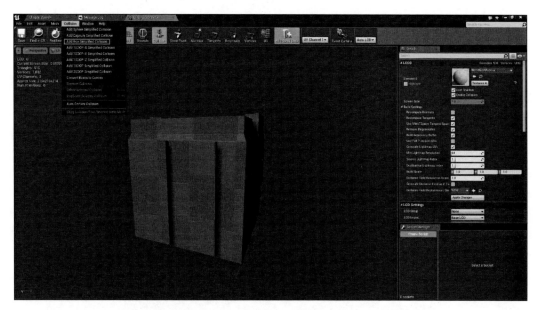

Select the Collision menu and choose Add Simple Box Collision

Lets see how Collision can be added to our object:

1. Make sure the **Collision** option is turned on along the top of the viewport. This will make any collision primitives we create visible.

2. Click the **Collision** menu option in the menu bar along the top of the screen. From here we will want to select the simplest shape that fits our needs. Since our crate is really just a box, we will select **Add Simple Box Collision**. You should now see a box outlined in green around the crate.

The next thing we need to do is select a material to add to our crate. Any of the materials available in the **Content Browser** can be used:

Adding a material to our box using the Details panel

1. Go back to the **Content Browser** and navigate to the **Materials** folder inside the **Starter Content** folder.

2. Click on the material you would like to use for the crate. I selected **M_Metal_Copper**.

3. With the material highlighted, go back to the **Static Mesh** editor and click the small arrow next to the material sphere in the **LOD 0** section of the Details panel. Whenever you see a small arrow like that in the Unreal Engine, clicking will allow you to use whatever you have selected in the **Content Browser**.

4. Your material will appear on your crate. Feel free to try a few different options to find what you think works best.

For our next game asset that we will create later in this book, we will use a custom material that will really make the object stand out. Once we have the material setting complete, there is only one more setting that we need to change. Unreal likes to generate its own UV channel for storing lighting information. However, back in *Chapter 3, It's Time to Customize!*, we created our own using Blender's Lightmap Pack feature, and we want to tell Unreal to use it, since ours is quite a bit better:

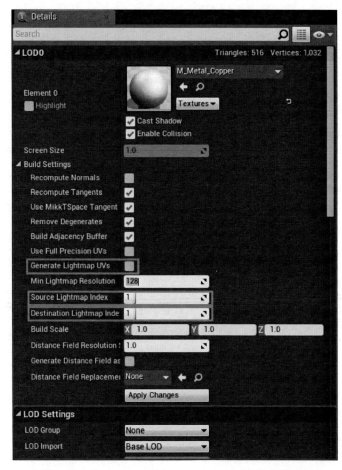

Telling Unreal to use our Lightmap we created within Blender

Here's how you can generate a Lightmap for your object:

1. Under the **LOD 0** section of the Details panel, find the **Generate Lightmap UVs** option and turn it off. This tells Unreal that we do not want it to create its own UV channel for lighting information.

2. Find the **Source Lightmap Index** setting. This tells Unreal which UV map to use when doing light calculations. Change this setting to 1.

3. Finally, go to the **Destination Lightmap Index** and change this to 1 as well. This tells Unreal to record the light and shadow information on the UV channel that we created.

Done! Our crate is ready for use:

The final crate inside our level. Congratulations!

Take a few minutes and replace a few of the cubes in the cargo bay with our new game asset. To really add some variation, try scaling a few of them up or down. Once the area is decorated to your liking, remember to save your level and press the **Build** button. Now drop into your level and check out the space!

Summary

In this chapter, we took a look at the process of getting our game asset out of Blender and into Unreal using the FBX file format. FBX is a file format used in the game industry that is popular for its ability to not only hold information about an object's geometry, but also information regarding textures, materials, and animation. We exported our FBX file from Blender and imported it into Unreal using the content browser. Once imported, the object still needed a collision mesh and materials. Finally, we were able to drop the crate into our level and replace many of our basic primitives with our brand new game asset. Congrats on completing your first trip through the art pipeline for your game! Before we get started with the next level, take some time and see if there is another game asset you would like to create and really add some more depth to the cargo ship we created. In the next chapter, the ship has taken us to a new level where the player will encounter new dangers and you will encounter new design challenges. Let's press on!

Taking This Level Up a Notch

5

Now that we have experienced the art pipeline for Unreal, let's kick our level design up a notch. In this chapter and the following chapters, we will be using the same process that we used previously, but we will be incorporating additional elements such as more level scripting, win conditions, animated game assets, and more. We will be further developing the story for our game and communicating to the player through level design and environment choices. The result will be a second level that builds off the survival horror feel we started building on the cargo ship. In this chapter, we will cover the following topics:

- Planning a more complex level
- Whiteboxing a level for better asset creation
- Level design principles
- Advanced scripting techniques
- Win and loss conditions

Planning a more complex level

With the cargo ship level, we introduced the player to a sci-fi world in which a mystery crate becomes a gateway to greater adventure. As we move on to a second level, we need to answer a few questions:

- Where did that cargo ship come from?
- What clue did that crate provide?
- What dangers lurk behind the next corner?

For me, the answers came from my entertainment influences. I am an avid reader of science fiction, as well as cerebral horror by authors like *H.P Lovecraft*. As a gamer, I enjoy games such as Dead Space, Mass Effect, and FEAR. So to pull from those influences, my thoughts turned to the crate containing some artifact plundered from an ancient race. This artifact somehow caused the disappearance of the crew of our cargo ship. However, an inspection of the crate left us with a clue: the name of an import/export broker based on a mining station not far from where the player found the abandoned freighter. Heading back to the bridge, the player sets a course for the space station.

Like all good things, we will start this level with a sketch on paper:

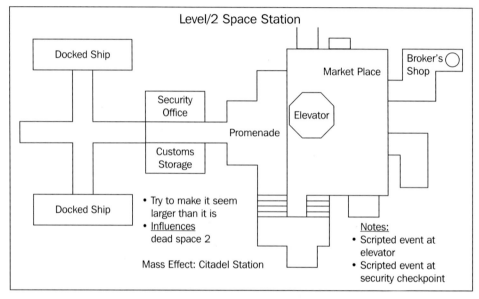

Just like our cargo ship, we start our space station on paper

For the space station, our design is centered on communicating the story to the player and providing a tense and foreboding atmosphere. Like the cargo ship they arrive on, the station is completely empty of any other human life. However, the area provides us as designers with ample opportunity to tell a story through scripted events.

Looking at our map, we can plan ahead and designate different areas as points where we can increase the player's sense of tension and direct the player toward the ultimate goal, the broker's stall in the marketplace. Since we want to avoid obvious clues such as signs and text prompts, we can designate some areas on our map for scripted events. These are areas where we will use **Blueprints** to communicate to the player and give clues as to the next step of the story. In a space station, these might be automated announcements over the PA system (audio clues), collapsing corridor sections due to damage (using triggered particle events), or creating vistas for the player to marvel at that also highlight the next goal (using level geometry). Let's take a look at the map. The player starts in the landing bay and has to progress through the airlock and security check. Here, we could use light, sounds, and some particle systems to create a malfunction that the player has to escape. Not deadly by any means, but it does communicate that there are no station staff present and that routine maintenance might have not been done in a while. Next, the player walks on to a promenade walkway. This could be an opportunity to present the player with a vista of the larger space station and highlight the location of the broker's shop down below. This communicates to the player that they need to find a way down to the market and makes them think that the level is much larger than the playable area. The player will then move over to the elevator, but this will malfunction as well and crash to the bottom of the shaft and force the player to take the stairs. When they finally enter the broker's stall, they should be on edge and ready for anything. Feel free to create your own interpretations of our scripted events and even add a few more.

Now let's move on to whiteboxing.

In this chapter, I will talk more about design principles and leave the actual whiteboxing to you, the reader. After working through *Chapter 2, Starting Our First Project*, I feel you have a strong foundation and can handle laying out the level.

Whiteboxing a level for better asset creation

Back in *Chapter 2, Starting Our First Project*, we used a method called whiteboxing to construct a mockup of our level. There are two reasons for this. First, we want to create a simple mock up for testing purposes with our target player base. Second, we want to get a good idea of how large to build our custom game assets, as well as where to put them. Through this process we quickly end up with a working prototype. For this level, we will be doing the same thing but we will also be paying attention to where we want the player to go and how they get there. This means using **blocking volumes**.

Blocking volumes are essentially invisible walls in your level. Designers use them to make sure players don't get stuck in certain parts of the level and to ensure that players don't just jump over a railing and miss an important scripted event. In our case, we want the player to not be able to fall into the space station's docking area or just jump over the promenade railing. One would result in getting stuck (and we would just have to kill them to get them unstuck) and the other would result in the player skipping our scripted elevator event. By using blocking volumes, we can guarantee the player a smooth gaming experience.

> It is important to consider when and where to use blocking volumes and to use them sparingly. We have all played games where an invisible wall has blocked an area that looks like it should otherwise be accessible. I still remember the frustration…

Let's add a blocking volume so that the player can't just jump the railing:

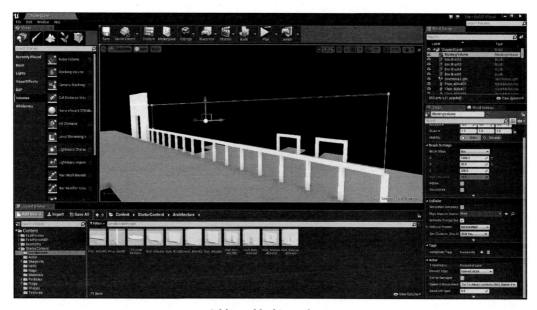

Adding a blocking volume

Blocking volumes are placed into our level much in the same way as BSP brushes:

1. Inside Unreal, click on the **Volumes** tab located in the **Modes** panel.
2. Select **Blocking Volume** and drag one into the level.

3. The default shape is a box. Let's adjust it to create an effective barrier to jumping off the promenade. In the **Brush** section of the **Details** panel, change the **X** to `1600`, change the **Y** to `30`, and keep the **Z** at `200`.

4. Move the shape to line up with the top of the railing.

Blocking volumes can also be used as the collision mesh for assets we create. For example, we often use the column asset in the **Architecture** folder to represent a pillar or similar floor-to-ceiling piece. Using a box shaped blocking volume, we can have whatever custom asset we create take up the same space while being able to create a truly custom shape, such as a pillar made of tentacles.

Another technique we can use during whiteboxing is using subtraction brushes with **BSP** to create custom shapes. BSP is something that we are familiar with. When we drop a box BSP brush into the level it creates a box. This defaults to using an additive brush and creates the shape within our level. The **Details** panel allows us to change the general size of the box but not much else.

Subtractive brushes are the exact opposite:

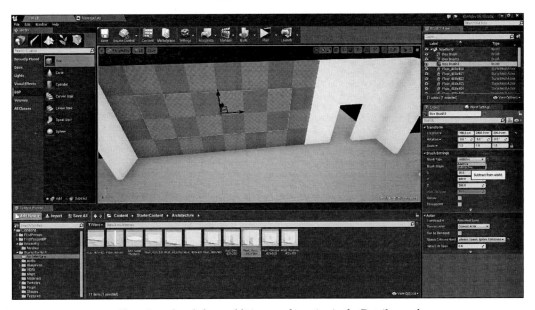

Changing a brush from additive to subtractive in the Details panel

A subtractive brush allows us to use the shape of a brush just like a cookie cutter to create doorways, holes, and more. Remember, this only works with additive and subtractive BSP brushes. You cannot use a subtractive brush to cut a hole in a static mesh.

Let's create a window for our security checkpoint:

1. Click on the **BSP** tab of the **Modes** panel and drag a **Box** into our level. In the **Details** panel, change the **X** to 20, **Y** to 800 so it will cover the space of two of our wall sections, and **Z** to 400 to fit the same vertical space as our wall section.

2. Fit the new brush into the section of the security checkpoint where we would like to have the window.

3. Drag another BSP **Box** into our level from the **Modes** panel. For this brush, we will set the **X** to 30 so it's a bit wider than our wall, **Y** to 600, and **Z** to 200.

4. Lastly, change the **Brush Type** from **Additive** to **Subtractive**:

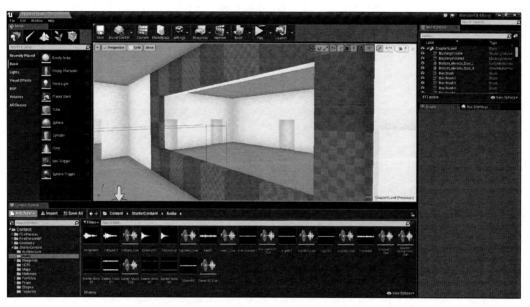

The final result of using our subtractive brush. Now we have a window!

5. Drag this brush so that it intersects our wall brush. This should create just the hole we want. Remember that if you want to copy this brush to use in other parts of the level that you must select both brushes to get the right effect.

Level design principles

When building game levels, understanding how to use the tools is important, but it is not the only thing a great level designer needs to know. The game level communicates with the player, telling them about the story and the setting, but also about goals, options, and other game information. I once heard a great presentation by a designer who had worked for many years building levels in the game industry. He mentioned that a player should be able to navigate a level with the game HUD turned off, relying only on the clues they find in the design of the level. For the player to be able to do this, the level must be built cleanly and efficiently, using clear sight lines and vistas to direct the player to the end goal. Since hearing this, I have attempted to bring these ideas into every level I create.

Let's talk about some of these points:

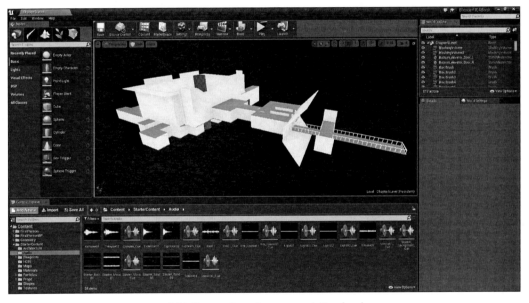

A bird's eye view of our space station level

Building levels that are clean and efficient sounds great, but what does that really mean? A clean level is free of distraction and extra areas that serve no real purpose to the story, environment, or level goals. Players can find these areas confusing and spend time searching for their importance when really there isn't any. When designing and building our levels, always ask yourself if each section of the level adds something to the player experience or if it is just a distraction there to add complexity to a level. Efficiency is important as well. Game design has many constraints: hardware constraints such as memory and processing speed, budget constraints, time constraints, and production constraints. It is important as the designer to maximize how you use your resources to create the most engaging player experience possible. For small game developers like ourselves, this can mean spending our time efficiently and finding ways to cut corners without sacrificing quality:

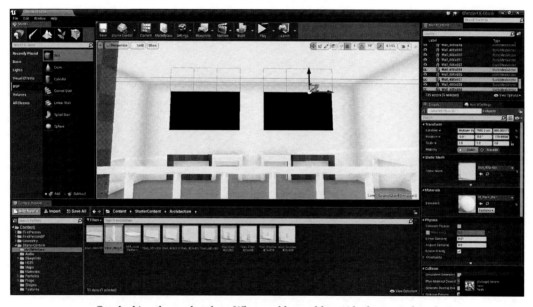

Overlooking the marketplace. What could we add outside those windows?

When building a level, it is also important to take into account what the player is seeing while navigating each section. The player's sight lines present them with options for navigating the spaces we design and we can use them to steer players through the paths that we intend. This will ensure that the player experiences everything in the way that we designed it. In our space station design, we restricted the paths the player can see as they progress through the level. When they enter the station, they are only aware of one path into the security checkpoint where they experience our scripted event. They are then provided with a sight line that leads them to a beautiful vista of the outside environment and the station's marketplace.

Here, they are free to do a bit of exploring of all they have seen:

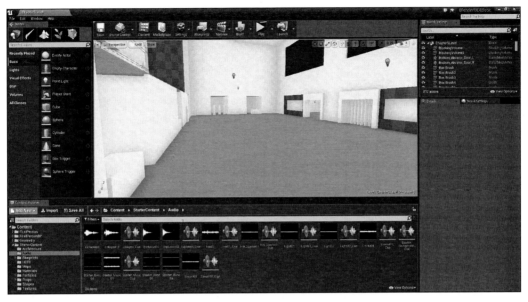

Exploring the marketplace. A great space for players!

Our player is also shown the ultimate goal of the level, the smoldering remains of the broker's shop, ready to be explored at their leisure. To sum things up, sight lines are a powerful tool that can control a player's progress, present them with options, and empower them to reach the level's goal.

Now one more reminder: as you whitebox the level, remember to have family, friends, and your intended audience playtest it for you. Their insight is valuable and can increase the chances of your game being successful!

Advanced scripting techniques

With the level whitebox nearly complete, it's time to start thinking about those scripted events. Scripting level events can add immensely to any level and can be as simple as triggered sounds or particle effects, or as complicated as fully scripted cutscenes or minigames. Unreal 4 gives us the ability to visually program these sequences using the flexible Blueprint system. We've used Blueprint before for simple doors and elevators back in *Chapter 2, Starting Our First Project*. Now we will build on that knowledge to design and program flexible scripted events.

So how do we start? Designing a scripted event is not unlike our animations systems we have built before. Each one starts with an event that causes several different actions to fire in a sequence. The trick is to be able to logic out the sequence so that we get the desired effect with the player. For example, the average game explosion has a few different actions:

1. Wait for the target object to take damage.
2. Once damage reaches a certain amount, create a radius of damage and fire the smoke, spark, fire, and explosion particle emitters.
3. Play explosion sound!
4. Use the flying particles as cover to delete the original object.
5. Spawn a damaged version of the original asset in its place.

Just like the explosion described here, any event can be broken down into specific events and simulated. So let's think about what our security checkpoint event needs. We need the player to feel threatened and to convey a sense of panic. I think we can do this by trying a few different things that together will have the desired effect. Here are some ideas in no particular order:

- Flash the lights
- Fill the room with smoke
- Sparks!
- Some kind of loud noise
- Slam the doors shut
- Slam the windows shut
- Fire!

 Brainstorming using sticky notes is a great way to come up with ideas like this very quickly. The sticky notes make the ideas movable so that you can easily organize them into any order you choose.

Now there's a few great ideas! The next step is to arrange them into a logical order that can be programmed. Computers can't do anything we haven't specifically spelled out for them, so we have to be pretty clear about our instructions. Here is just one example of how I might order the instructions:

1. Animate the doors and windows closed.

2. Some kind of loud noise.

3. Fire the smoke emitter.

4. Fire the spark emitter.

5. Play some clue to the player to let them know what to do to get out.

Seems like a pretty solid plan. The next step would be to add those additional elements to our level. Each entrance to the security checkpoint hallway needs a door, each window needs a shutter, and so on.

Let's build the doors first:

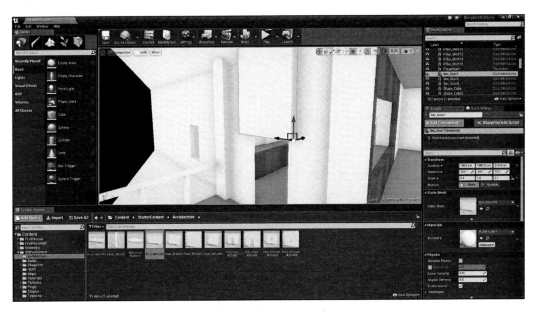

Building the first security door

1. For the three security doors that slam down, I grabbed a **Wall_400x200** piece from the **Architecture** folder and adjusted the **Scale** of the **X** to 0.4 and the **Z** to 1.1. I then changed the name for each to Sec_Door1, Sec_Door2, and Sec_Door3. Remember to also set the **Mobility** property to Movable.

2. I positioned each door above each door frame so that it can slam down during the event:

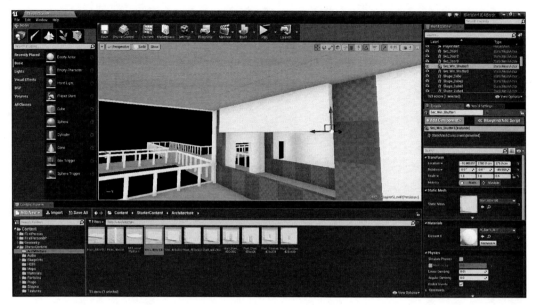

Building the security shutters

3. For the two security window shutters, I used a **Wall_400x400** piece and adjusted the Scale property of the x to `1.5` and the z to `0.5`. I changed their names to `Sec_Win_Shutter1` and `Sec_Win_Shutter2` to make them easy to identify and set their **Mobility** to **Movable**.

Time to add a few more details to really make this area perfect:

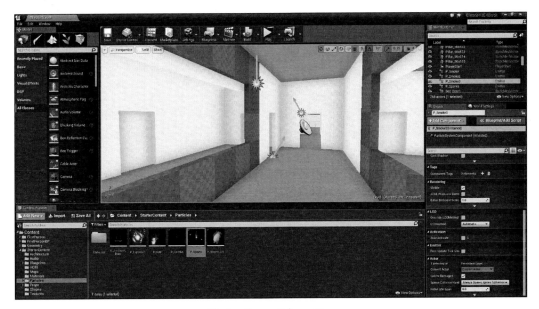

Placing the particle emitters

1. Particle emitters are points in space that emit light, sparks, or even static meshes if we want them to. They are created using Unreal's Cascade Particle Editor, though the **Starter Content** folder has some great ones we can use in the **Particles** sub-folder. Here I used a **P_Smoke** emitter at each door and one **P_Sparks** emitter near the window on the left. For all of them, I turned off the **Auto Activate** option in the **Details** panel to give us control of when they fire.

A trap like this is great, but we still need some way for the player to escape:

A view of the security office

2.   After a couple seconds, let's have the door to the security room malfunction and explode, allowing the player to reach the security override button! I have placed a couple of **Point Lights** above the door, one red and one green, that can indicate the door is opening (turn off the **Visible** property for the red light in the **Details** panel) and have built the override button using a Box Trigger and a **SM_MatPreviewMesh_02** from the **Props** folder of the **Content Browser**. To make sure that clue is clear to the player I have placed a **Text Render** object above the button reading *"Disengage Security Lockdown"*.

With all the pieces in place we are ready to script our event. Open the **Level Blueprint** by pressing the **Blueprints** button above the viewport and selecting **Open Level Blueprint**. For this level of scripting, we are also going to go up to the **Window** button in the toolbar and turn on the **Palette** window. This gives us access to a customizable **Favorites** list of nodes and the **Find a Node** search box, a great tool when constructing new Blueprint sequences:

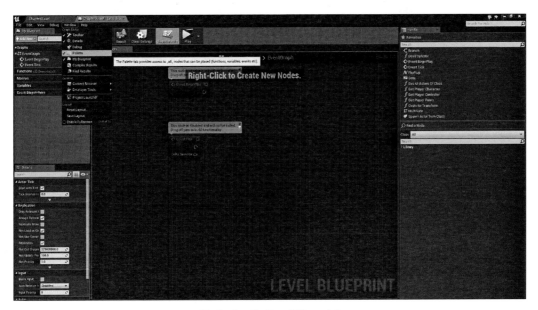

Beginning the Level Blueprint

1. Select both of the default nodes located in the Blueprint area and press *Delete*. We won't need them for this sequence.

2. We need an event to start our sequence off. Back in the level, place a **Box Trigger** in the security checkpoint, about halfway down the hallway. Set its **Box Extents** property to be large enough to make missing it impossible. This will make the player trigger the security lockdown after they have completely entered the hallway. Inside the **Level Blueprint**, *Right-click* and select **Add Event for Trigger Box**, select **Collision**, and then select **Add OnActorBeginOverlap**. Remember that your trigger box number may vary from mine:

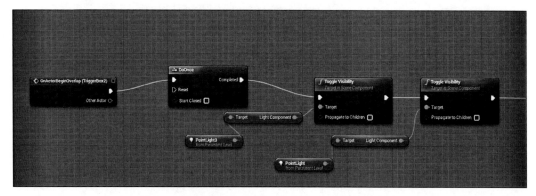

The complete Blueprint for swapping our colored lights

3. Now, we need to change the warning light color. For this we are going to add a couple different nodes. In the search box of the **Find a Node** section of the **Palette** pane, type in Do Once. This node works like a gate and ensures that anything after it only runs once. Here, we use it to make sure that the trigger we use to start the sequence cannot be set off more than once. Next, search for the **Toggle Visibility** node. Drag two of them into the Blueprint and connect them as shown. The targets for these nodes will be our red and green lights. We want to make sure we are showing the light we want and hiding the light we don't want:

Gathering our initial locations on our doors and windows

4. Time to slam the doors and windows shut! This part looks a bit complicated but is actually just like something we did in *Chapter 2, Starting Our First Project*. We are going to use a **Timeline** to shut all of the security doors we created at the same time. The first thing we need to do is save the initial locations of all the things we are going to animate. Without this step, the doors and windows would slam down then keep going right through the floor! To stop that from happening, we animate the door's position from its initial position. First, create some vector variables to hold the data for the three security doors and two windows. Next, we will build a special sequence to handle collecting that data. Start with an **Event BeginPlay** event and connect it to a **Set** node for each variable. Then connect a **Get Actor Location** node to each **Set**, with each door and window as a target. This will get the location of each piece and then set it as the variable so that we can animate it in the next step:

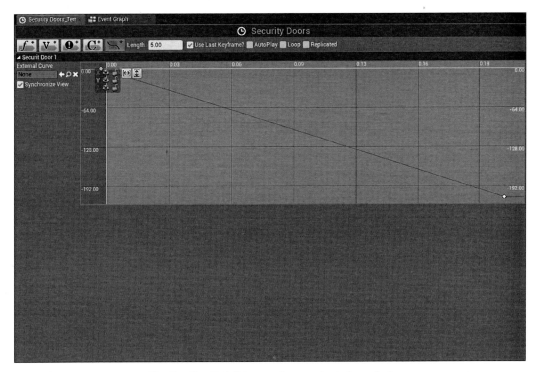

The timeline that slides our doors and windows shut

5. Now add the **Timeline** node and double click it to open it up. We want to slide our doors and window shutters down into place using a **Vector Track**. Remember that in a **Vector Track**, we can animate all three axes of movement, but we only want to use the Z axis here, so it will take a bit of sorting. Hold the *Shift* key and click on the red line. This will add a keyframe to the X-axis. Now click on the new keyframe and drag it out of the way. Now do the same on the green line and drag the Y-axis out of the way. This leaves us with the blue line, the z axis. Create a keyframe there and make sure its time and value are both set to 0. Add a second keyframe and set the time to something fast. I used 0.25. Set the value to -210. This will slide them down into place, blocking our player's escape. After creating your keyframes for the Z-axis, feel free to delete the keyframes on the other two axes by clicking them and pressing the *Delete* key. You can also lock and hide these axes by using the buttons located in the upper left portion of the graph. Be sure to select the **Last Keyframe** checkbox as well. This tells the **Timeline** to stop at the last keyframe in the sequence:

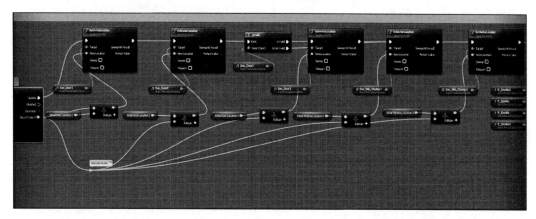

Using the Set Actor Location node to move all of these doors and windows

6. To finish off the animation, we need to connect a **Set Actor Location** node to the **Update** portion of our **Timeline** for each element that needs to be animated. Each of these nodes needs the appropriate target as well as a location to animate to. Just like in *Chapter 2, Starting Our First Project*, we will get the initial location of each element using our variables and add it with a **Vector + Vector** node to the **Vector Track** from the **Timeline**. Set each node up just like I have in the image. Near the bottom, I used a **Reroute** node to create all the connections to the **Vector + Vector** nodes. These can be used to redirect your connections if they start to get lost or separate out a connection into multiple wires so that it can be used multiple times. *Right-click* to open the menu and find the **Reroute** node near the bottom:

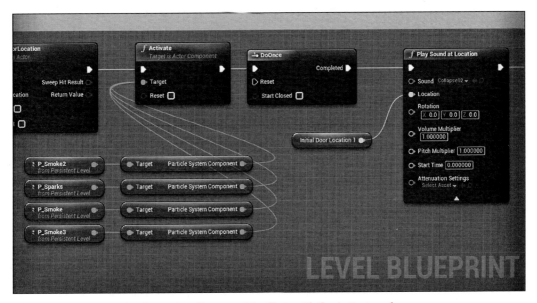

Activating all our particle effects with the Activate node

7. Light the fireworks! Time to activate all of our particle effects. We do this using a… You guessed it! An **Activate** node! Search for this node using the **Find a Node** section and drag it into the Blueprint. The targets will be each of the particle effects. The targets can be created easily by going back to the level and holding the *ctrl* key while selecting each one. Back in the Blueprint, *Right-click* and select **Create Reference to 4 Selected Actors**. Plugging them in to the **Activate** node's **Target** will create the translation nodes (the nodes that say **Target** and **Particle System Components**):

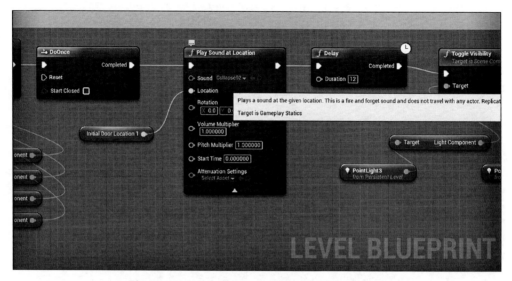

Playing our sound effects using Play Sound at Location

8. Next we will use **Play Sound at Location** to play our **Sound Cue**. This node is very straightforward and plays a sound chosen from the **Content Browser** at a location that we determine. Find this node and connect to our existing sequence. For my sound, I chose **Collapse02** from the **Audio** portion of the **Starter Content** folder. For my location, I used one of the initial locations we had already stored in a variable:

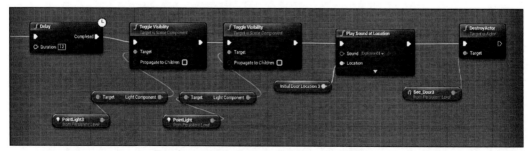

Toggling security lights and destroying the door

9. We are in the home stretch for this sequence. Using a **Delay** node, let's destroy the door to the security office and swap the lights. A **Delay** node will stop the execution of the sequence for a predetermined amount of time. Playtest the sequence to get a feel for how long you want the player to wait. The longer you have the **Delay**, the more tension and panic it creates! After much testing, I went with 12 seconds. More seemed too long. Less seemed too fast. Next, use a couple of **Toggle Visibility** nodes on our lights again to bring back our green light. This visual cue will let the player know where to go next. To give our player an audio cue, play the **Explosion01** sound at the location of the door that leads to the security office. Finally, grab a **Destroy** node from the **Find a Node** section. In game terms, **Destroy** is just a fancy word for delete (I think it sounds better). Use this to delete the door:

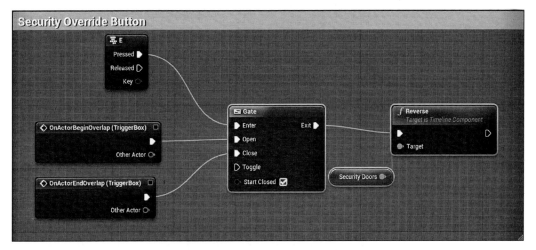

Programming the security override button

10. Lastly, let's program the button for the security override. The event is actually three events. The first two involve the trigger we created to make the button work. Select the level and create an **OnActorBeginOverlap** event and an **OnActorEndOverlap** event. The last event we need is a keyboard input for the *E* key. This can be found by typing `Input E` into the **Find a Node** search box. These will all be wired into a **Gate** node, just like we did for our elevator back on the cargo ship. This will require the player to stand within the trigger to open the **Gate** and make the *E* key work. To finish this sequence, wire the **Exit** part of the **Gate** into a **Timeline Reverse** node. The target can be found by dragging a wire off the target portion of the **Reverse**, opening up **Class**, then your level, and finally, selecting the **Timeline** used to control the security doors and windows.

Time to test! Playtest this section of the level and make sure everything is working. Feel the drama! Now it's time to script our elevator sequence. Compared to the security checkpoint, this one is easy!

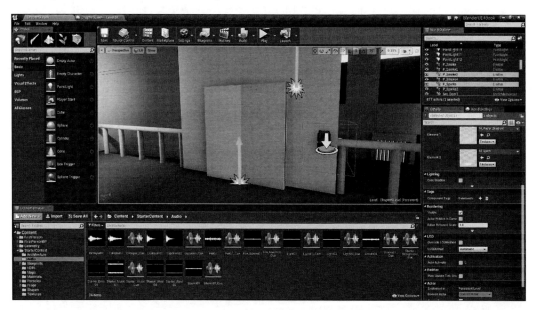

Setting up the components for the elevator sequence

The elevator sequence works much like a shorter version of the security checkpoint sequence. When the player walks into a trigger, animate one elevator door, turn on a few particle emitters, and play a sound. Let's get started:

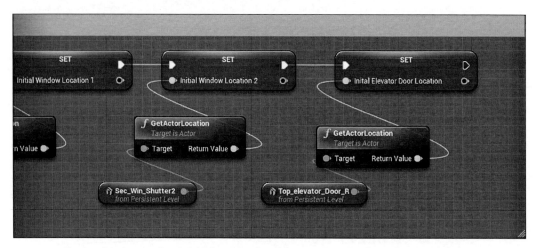

Getting the elevator door's initial position by adding onto our level initialization sequence

1. Since we will be using a **Timeline** for this sequence, create a vector variable to hold the initial location of the door we plan to animate and set it using the same technique we used to get the initial location of the security doors.

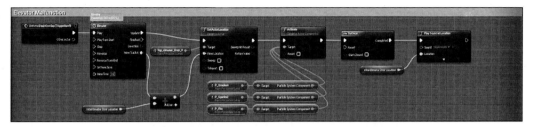

Scripting the elevator sequence. Connect the nodes in this order: On Overlap, Timeline,
Set Actor Location, Activate, Do Once, Play Sound at Location

2. The event that kicks this one off is an **OnActorBeginOverlap**, using the trigger in front of the elevator buttons.

3. Next, create a **Timeline** to move one of the doors just a bit, to make the player think they are opening.

4. Use the **Activate** node to activate the smoke and sparks at the elevator door. I also added a fire emitter at the bottom of the elevator shaft and opened the doors down there a bit to give the player a view of what could have happened to them once they get down to the marketplace.

5. I then used a **Do Once** and a **Play Sound at Location** node to have an explosion sound play. **Do Once** makes sure the audio doesn't try to loop and ruin the experience we are going for.

All done! Test the sequence to make sure it has the emotional effect that you want. Feel free to tweak the different particle effects, sounds, and timings until it feels right for you and your playtesters. In the next section, we will talk about win conditions and how to connect our two levels together.

Win conditions

At this point in the book we have two whitebox levels, complete with a starting point and an end goal in each one. We have also constructed a bit of narrative that strings the two together. In this section, I will show you how to use Blueprints to connect the two levels and allow a player to go from the cargo ship level to the space station by investigating the crate. In the end, we will have the skeleton of a game demo that could definitely be expanded on with additional art and gameplay to create a full game.

To connect the two levels, we will have to go back to the cargo ship and add a triggered event to the crate we placed there that allows the player to investigate it. This trigger will then allow the player to load to the space station level to continue the story:

Connecting our cargo ship level to the space station level

1. Open the cargo ship level and add two things: A **Box Trigger** around the crate we created and a **Text Render** with a message saying to press the *E* key to investigate it.

2. Open up the **Level Blueprint** and find an area to start our sequence. Click on the new **Box Trigger** in the level and create an **OnActorBeginOverlap** event and an **OnActorEndOverlap** event. Also use the **Find a Node** tool in the **Palette** pane to grab an input **E** event:

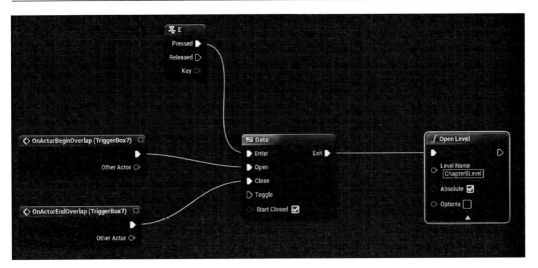

Programming the button that triggers the level transition

3. By now, this sequence should be familiar to you. Connect the events we just created to a **Gate** node to create an event that only works when you are within the trigger area.

4. Lastly, add the **Open Level** node. This can be found using the **Find a Node** search box. This node will transport the player to our new space station level. In the **Level Name** field, type in the name of the space station level. Make sure the name you enter is correct or the node will not work.

Now playtest the cargo ship and investigate the unusual readings coming from the crate. This should take you to the start of the space station level. If this were a completed game, we might have a loading screen or some audio explaining the story as we go. Keep ideas like this in mind! There is always time for polish and improvements later.

Does everything feel like it's starting to come together?

Summary

In this chapter, we began the process of whiteboxing a much larger level than our previous one, a mysterious space station that may hold clues as to why the crew of the cargo ship disappeared. During the prototype phase, we also created two scripted events. The first one takes place at the security checkpoint coming in from the docking bay and is designed to create tension and increase the feeling that something is wrong on the station. The second one is a malfunctioning elevator that tells the player that something must have happened and certain death could be lurking right around the corner. But what does the player find in the back of the import/export broker's shop? In the next chapter, we will head back to Blender to design an answer to that question and create a new mysterious and complex game asset for our level.

6
Monster Assets – The Level Totally Needs One of These

The mystery continues! At this point, the player has made it back to the import/export broker's shop in the Marketplace section of our space station, but what do they see? We could go a few different ways here, such as an interdimensional portal, advanced military hardware, or even something mystical. One of my favorite authors has always been *H.P. Lovecraft*, a horror fiction writer from the early 1900s. His short stories often revolved around themes of forbidden knowledge, cults, hidden secrets, and madness-inducing horrors, and he often talked about Elder Gods from beyond the stars. What if our intrepid hero stumbled upon an Artifact from another world with ties to just such a nameless star god that devours sanity? Surely, an importer on a busy space station could make a fortune selling such a thing to a collector. Why would he care about the stories of madness attached to it? That would only add to the allure of the purchase. In this chapter, we will cover the following topics:

- Designing our asset: inspiration and concept art
- Advanced tools: Subdivide, Knife, Bridge Edge Loops, and more
- Using multiple shapes within Blender
- The importance of keeping track of polygon and triangle counts

Designing our asset – inspiration and concept art

As I mentioned earlier, from *H.P. Lovecraft* short stories, particularly those of the popular Cthulhu Mythos, are some of my favorite weird tales. In these stories, intrepid investigators come into contact with objects and creatures born of madness, along with the servants of dark and terrible gods. Using this idea as inspiration, we once again turn to Google Images in search of more inspirational writings and images. A quick search provides interesting ideas. The Elder Gods are often depicted in art as otherworldly. Tentacles, screaming mouths, multiple eyes, uneven physiques, and more, are depicted, mixed with more human elements. So how might we take these ideas and incorporate them into a design for a game asset that will not look out of place on a space station in the far future?

Time to sketch our concept:

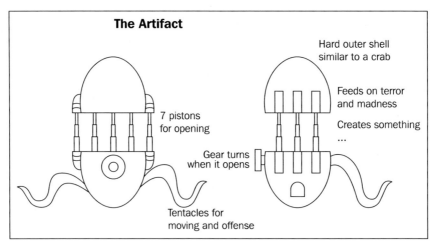

Sketch of the Artifact

My initial thoughts were to create some type of container, like a Pandora's Box, that when opened unleashes a sinister power that feeds on everyone around it. Instead of being a square, like a crate or box, I decided to create a container that was more egg-shaped. It would immediately stand out in the environment and draw the player to it. The Artifact should be able to be opened so that the player may accidentally unleash whatever is inside. The design incorporates some steampunk elements in its opening mechanism as a nod to the time period in which many of *H.P. Lovecraft's* written stories take place. Finally, there are also deep sea elements such as tentacle handles, a spiked crab shell exterior, and an all-seeing eye. This should definitely get the player's attention!

For this asset, we have to give some thought to how the object opens, as we will be animating these elements in Blender. In this design, the round elements turn and retract the pistons that hold the lid, allowing for the top to twist open. Each of these moving parts will be created, starting with a different base shape.

To make sure that it fits in the space we have inside the level, we will create the asset close to the size of the existing test asset that we used:

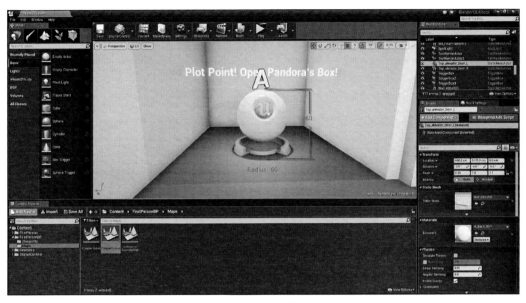

The test asset has a radius of 60 and a height of 60

Advanced tools: Subdivide, Knife, Bridge Edge Loops, and more

As we build this new asset, there are a few new tools that we need to be aware of that will allow us to increase the level of detail on the Artifact.

Now let's take a look at some new tools we will be using.

Subdivide tool

The **Subdivide** tool is a great tool that can be used to add more connecting lines and polygons to a section of a model to add detail. Use this tool by selecting the lines or polygons you wish to subdivide and clicking the **Subdivide** tool in the **Tools** pane. The number of connections may be adjusted by changing the **Number of Cuts** field in the lower-left corner of the screen:

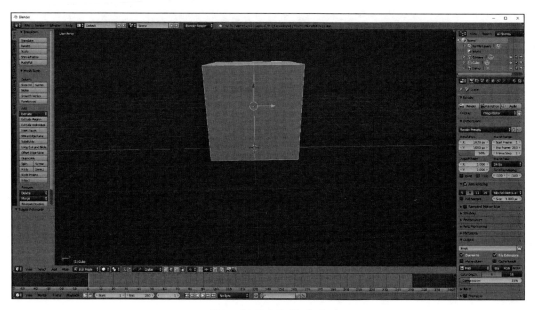

Using the Subdivide tool

Knife tool

The **Knife** tool can be used to make freehand cuts into the geometry of an object and is great for creating additional artistic detail on small parts of your model. To get started, click the **Knife** tool in the **Tools** pane, or press *K*. The cursor will change to a small knife. Click once to start the cut and then click each time you would like to add a point to the line. Hovering the mouse over an existing vertex will turn the cursor green and allow you to connect your new lines with the existing geometry. Press the *Spacebar* to finalize your cut, or *E* to start a new one:

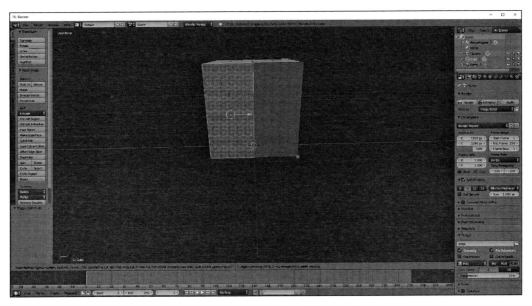

The Knife tool is great for adding detail

Bridge Edge Loops tool

The **Bridge Edge Loops** tool is an essential tool for creating new polygons by connecting two or more edges together. We will use it often after deleting old polygons to restructure the geometry into a more functional shape. Use it by selecting your lines in the **Line** selection mode, pressing *W* to open the **Specials** menu, and selecting **Bridge Edge Loops**:

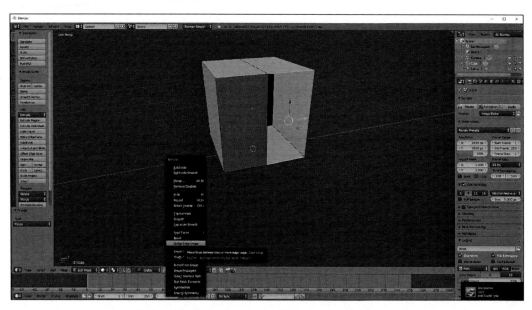

Bridge Edge Loops is great for filling in a hole in a shape

Triangulate modifier tool

The last thing I want to mention is something we will use after we have finished with the model. When we export an object out of Blender and bring it into Unreal, the game engine turns all of our nice polygons into triangles for its own purposes. Now, for the most part this won't be a problem. Unreal was able to handle our simple crate pretty well. However, the more complicated the object, the greater the chance that Unreal will mess it up when it imports the file. We can help this process along by triangulating our object before we export it from Blender. Adding the **Triangulate** modifier is done in the **Modifier** menu of the **Properties** pane. Remember that you must be in **Object** mode to apply any modifier:

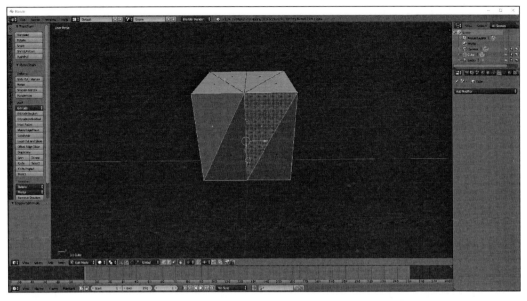

Triangulate is essential, since most game engines require game assets to be made from triangles anyway

With these additional tools we should be able to create an amazing Artifact. Time to start building!

Using multiple shapes within Blender

To begin building our object, we need to break our design down into its individual pieces and decide on a primitive shape to start building each part. The bottom section looks like a cylinder. The lid looks like the top portion of a sphere split in two. The gears and pistons that make up the locking mechanism definitely look like cylinders and the legs could start that way too.

[Don't forget to set up your file with the appropriate settings like we did in *Chapter 3, It's Time to Customize!*]

Now, let's start with a cylinder:

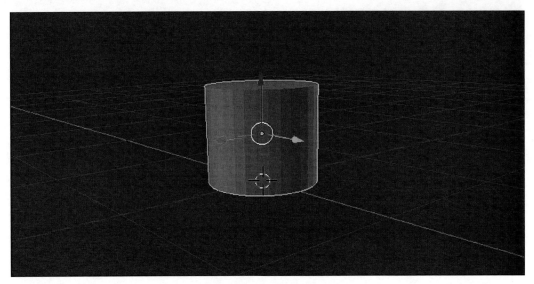

Starting with a cylinder

Let's start the build with the bottom of the object:

1. Delete the starting objects from the scene, if you have them. Go to the **Add** menu located at the bottom of the 3D viewport, go to **Mesh**, and select **Cylinder** from the options. In the bottom of the **Tools** pane, you can see the options for our newly created **Cylinder**. Set the **Sides** to 24 (using just enough sides to stay round), set the **Radius** to 60, and the **Depth** to 60. Remember that these are based on the measurements we took of our whitebox prop in Unreal.

2. Now move our newly created object up so that it looks like it's sitting on the grip. This will give our Artifact a good pivot point in Unreal:

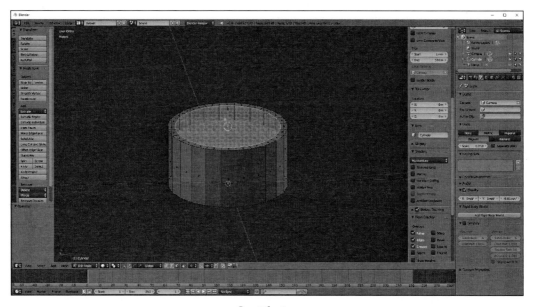

Inset the top

3. Time to start shaping this thing. Press *Tab* to go to **Edit** mode. Select the top polygon and use the **Inset** tool to start giving it an inside. I set my **Inset** value to about 7.10:

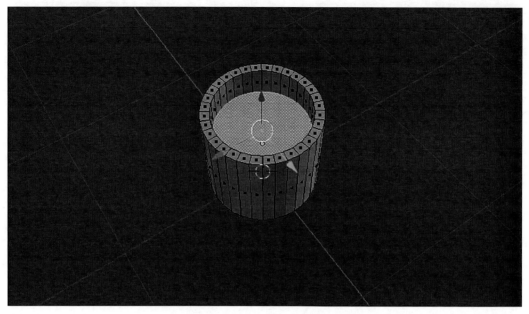

Use the Extrude to create the inside of the Artifact

4. Next, take the new polygon created by the **Inset** and **Extrude** it down into the base. Not too much; we want to give the illusion that it has a lot of space inside, but we don't want to push the polygon through the bottom.

5. Now let's taper the bottom a bit. Grab the bottom polygon of our cylinder and **Scale** it down a bit. Be careful not to let the inside polygon poke through the sides. I scaled it by 0.75.

6. But wait! We still need a flat section for the locking mechanisms and legs to connect to! We can achieve this effect by creating a new edge loop around the middle section and scaling it back out:

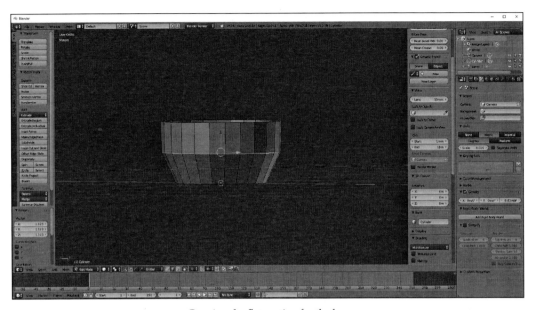

Creating the flat section for the legs

7. Change your selection to **Line** mode and select all the lines around the middle. This can be achieved by pressing *B* to do a window selection, rotating your view, and doing another window selection until you have selected all of the lines. With them selected, click on the **Subdivide** tool in the **Tools** pane. This will create our new loop. Now select all the lines that make up that loop and **Scale** it outward to again flatten out the upper part of our base:

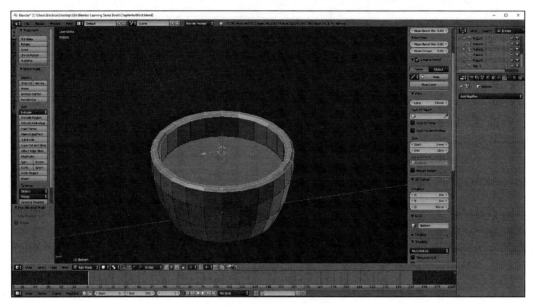

Beveling the edges

8. Let's round it out. Unlike the crate we created earlier, the shapes we are creating now are more rounded and organic. Select the lines that make up the inside and outside edges of the top of our Artifact. Press *W* to open up the **Specials** Menu and select **Bevel**. Using **Bevel** on an edge splits it into two edges. By using it on those two edge loops we can create a rounded element to our shape:

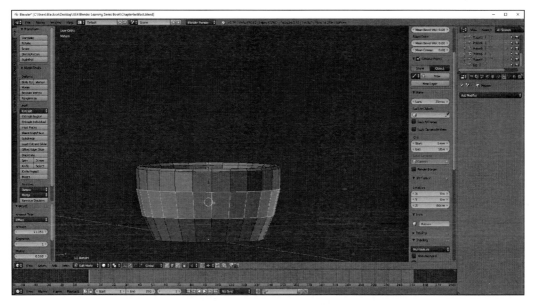

Bevel once again to round out the shape

Remember to be careful when using **Bevel**, we don't want the shape to turn itself inside out!

9. One more **Bevel** and we can call this part done. Select the edge loop we created in Step 6 and give it a **Bevel**. This will give the bottom portion a good round shape as well. What you should have now should look like the beginnings of a flower pot, a very sinister flower pot.

10. Looking at our sketch, the top portion looks similar to the bottom. We can save ourselves some time by duplicating the bottom piece and flipping it over:

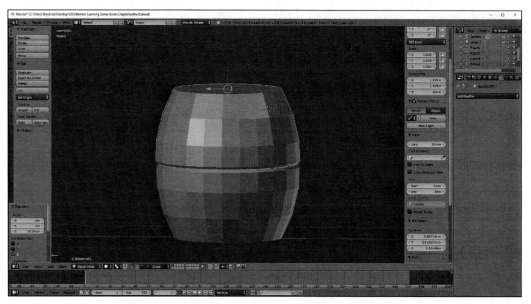

Duplicate the bottom to create our starting shape for the top

11. In **Object** mode, select the bottom piece and click **Duplicate**, or press *Shift* + *D*. This will create a copy, but it will start moving it in all directions and we want to keep our pieces aligned. Press *Z* to lock the movement to the Z-axis and move the copy up a bit. Now use the **Rotate** tool and press *X* to lock the rotation to around the *X*-axis. Finally, type in 180 and press *Enter* to flip it over:

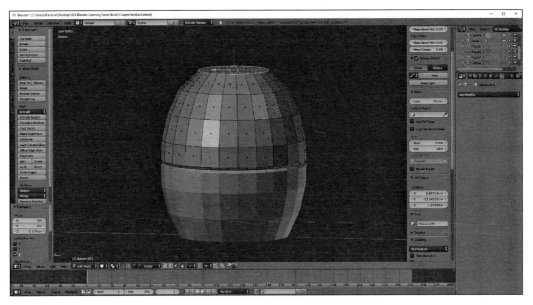

Elongating the top of the Artifact

12. Rounding out the top will give us the egg shape we are looking for. Grab the top polygon of our new lid and **Extrude** it out some more. Then **Scale** the new top polygon down a bit. It will start to look more rounded. Repeat this step once or twice more until you get the shape you desire.

The Artifact now has a bottom and a top section and is beginning to look a bit like our design drawing:

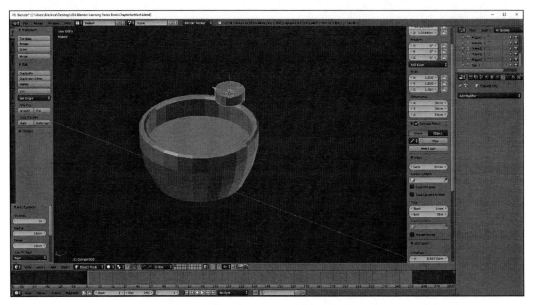

Starting the gear section with a cylinder

In the next few steps, we will build the first part of the lock, a gear that holds a talisman in its claws:

1. We need a basic shape to start this piece off with. Since a gear essentially has a round, flat shape, a cylinder should start us off quite nicely. In **Object** mode, click on the **Add** menu at the bottom of the 3D viewport, select **Mesh**, and choose **Cylinder** from the list. I created mine with 16 **Vertices**, a 15cm **Radius**, and a 10cm of **Depth**. Move it into position on the model and rotate it 90 degrees to sit it flat against the bottom portion of the Artifact. Part of the gear will be inside the Artifact.

2. Now that things are getting more complicated, let's use the **Scene Outliner** to name our objects and hide the ones we aren't working on. Click on the bottom portion of the Artifact. You will see in the **Scene Outliner** that it is named **Cylinder** and everything after that is **Cylinder.001**, and so on. If we double-click the name, we can rename the object whatever we wish. I have named my components `Bottom`, `Top`, and `Gear`. Names aren't super important here, but you should name them something you can recognize. You may also notice that each object in the **Scene Outliner** has an eye next to it. Clicking on this eye will cause it to close and will hide that object in the 3D viewport. This is a great way to work on different sections of a complex game asset without the other pieces getting in your way.

3. Now let's do an **Inset**:

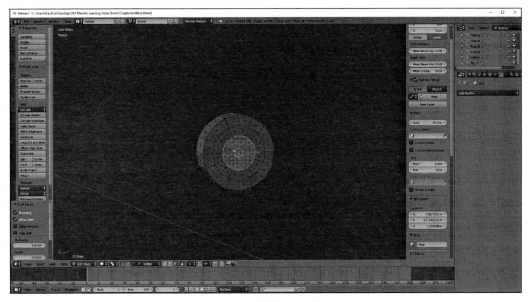

Using Inset to add detail to the gear

4. Heading into **Edit** mode, we can start shaping this cylinder into the gear we need. Hide the top and bottom portions of the Artifact so you can only see the piece we are working on. Select the front polygon and press *I* to **Inset** it. I did an **Inset** of 5cm. Then we are going to **Inset** it another 5cm. Once that is done, do the same thing to the back polygon:

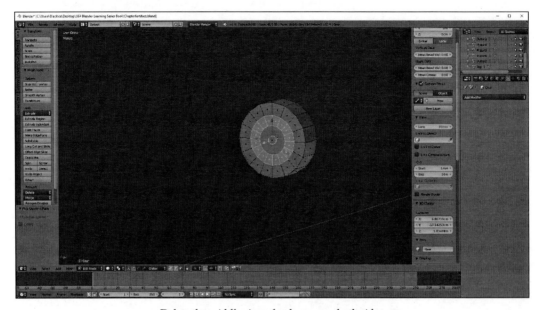

Delete the middle ring of polygons on both sides

5. Select the middle ring of polygons we just created and press *Delete*. When it asks what to delete, select **Faces** from the menu. Just as before, do the same for the back side:

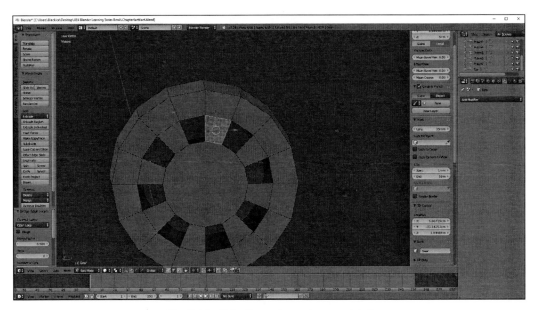

Use Bridge Edge Loops to create more detail

6. Time to use the **Bridge Edge Loops** tool! Starting at the 12 o'clock position, select the first line on the inner polygon and its corresponding line on the outer polygon. Press *W* and select **Bridge Edge Loops** tool. Look at that nice new polygon! Now do the same for every other line all the way around the circle. As before, do the same on the back side of the gear. In the next step, we will build the inside polygons of the gear:

Don't worry if something messes up when creating these new polygons. Just press *Ctrl + Z* to undo it and try again!

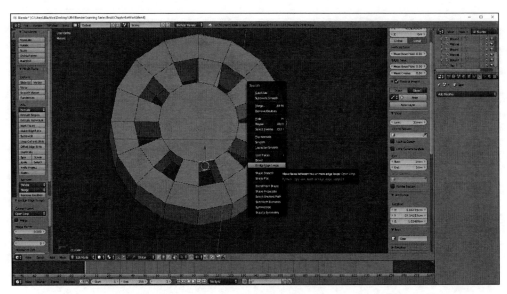

Using Bridge Edge Loops to create the inside portion of the gear shape

7. Adding the inside polygons to the arms of the gear is a four-step process. We need to use the **Bridge Edge Loops** tool to create four polygons in each hole to seal up the inside of the piece:

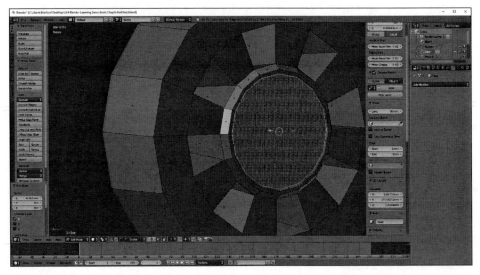

Extrude and scale to create more detail in the center of the gear

8. The center of the gear is meant to look like it is holding a medallion or talisman and is another multi-part operation done in small amounts. Select the center polygon on the front of the gear and **Extrude** it out. Next, scale it down a little bit to start creating a lip for the hole that it will sit in:

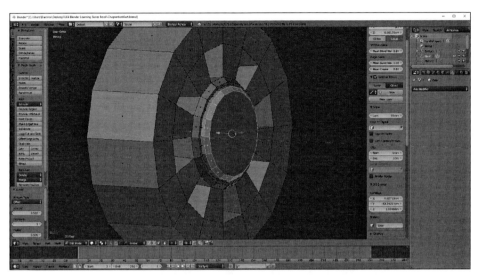

Extrude and bevel the center to finish out the details

9. Now, **Inset** the polygon to create the top part of the lip. Create the rest of the lip by extruding the polygon inward a bit and **Scaling** it down. Finally, **Extrude** out and **Bevel** the polygon to finish the shape:

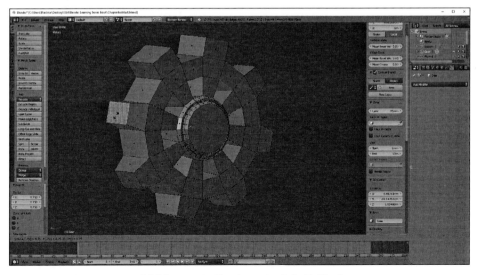

Add the gear teeth using extrude individual

10. What is a gear without teeth? To create the teeth, we **Extrude** the polygons around the outside of the gear that line up with the arms on the inside. We can select all of the polygons at once and select **Extrude Individual** from the **Tools** pane. This allows us to extrude each polygon so that the gear teeth are equal. After that, just **Scale** each polygon on the end of the teeth down a bit. I scaled each one by 0.75:

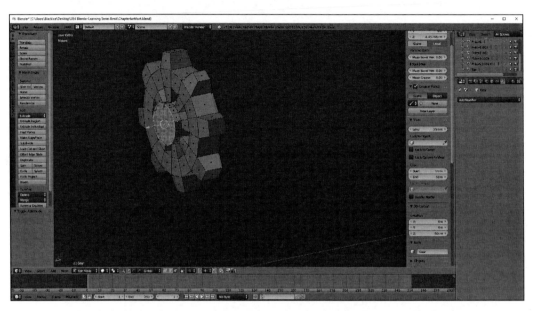

Extrude the back polygon out a bit to create a place for the gear to attach to the Artifact

11. Time for the finishing touch! Select the back polygon and **Extrude** it out to create a post on which the gear can spin. This will create a good contact point for the gear to mount on the bottom section of the Artifact.

To open, the Artifact uses pistons to raise the lid. The design calls for seven of them spaced around the bottom section of the object. We're going to cheat a little bit on this one and create just one piston, which we can just copy to create the other six.

There are two major things I've learned when it comes to 3D modelling. The first is that it's important to work smarter and not harder. The second is that sometimes we build things just to make them look cool!

Since the piston itself is round, we once again start with our old friend the cylinder. Let's get started!

1. Create yourself a new cylinder. I set mine to 32 **Vertices**, 3.75cm **Radius**, and a **Depth** of 15cm:

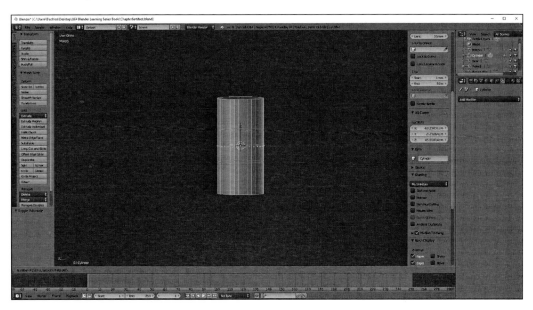

Start with a cylinder and use Loop, Cut, and Slide to add two new edge loops

2. To create a wider middle section, select all of the middle polygons and use the **Loop, Cut, and Slide** tool to add two new edge loops around the center. Click again to finalize the cut. Now click the **Extrude** dropdown in the Tools pane and select **Region (Vertex Normals)**. This will extrude all of the polygons out from the center evenly.

3. Let's round off the bottom. **Extrude** the bottom polygon of the piston and then use the **Bevel** tool on it. This should give us a nice rounded end:

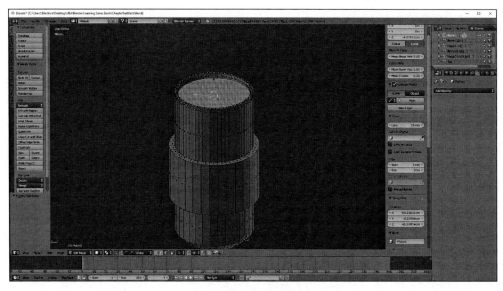

Adding a lip to the piston

4. For an added touch, give the top of the piston a lip, just like we did for the front of the gear. **Extrude** the top polygon just a little bit, then **Inset** it a little, and finally **Extrude** the polygon back down into the piston:

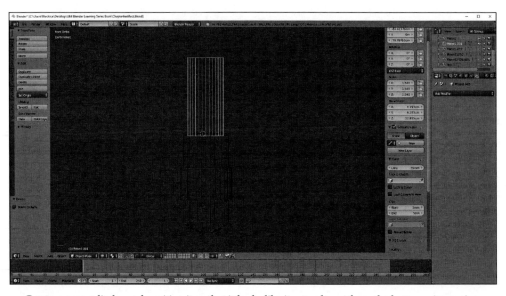

Create a new cylinder and position it so that it looks like it extends out from the bottom piston piece

5. Now the piston has to extend to raise the lid far enough so that whatever sinister thing is inside can get out. We can do this by creating a telescoping portion that lifts the lid. Now you may think that sounds difficult, but remember, work smarter not harder. We can create this portion by creating a second cylinder to extend out of the first part. Create a cylinder that is of 32 **Vertices**, 3 cm of **Radius**, and 13 cm of **Depth**. Line this up with the bottom portion of our piston. You can switch to a wireframe view by pressing Z to get a better view. Press Z again to go back to the solid view:

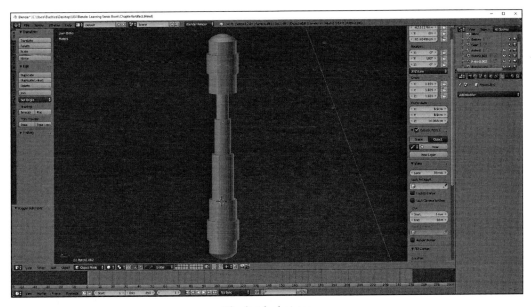

The finished piston

6. To raise it up high enough, we need to add a few more sections to the piston. Take the first portion and **Duplicate** it. Then move it upward to line up with the top of the last section. Finally scale it down to 0.75. To make the next section, rinse and repeat. What you get is three sections that, when moved down, fit neatly inside one another. When we animate the Artifact opening and closing, we will expand and compress the sections to give the illusion that it telescopes out.

7. To finish off the piston, **Duplicate** the first piece we created and make that the top:

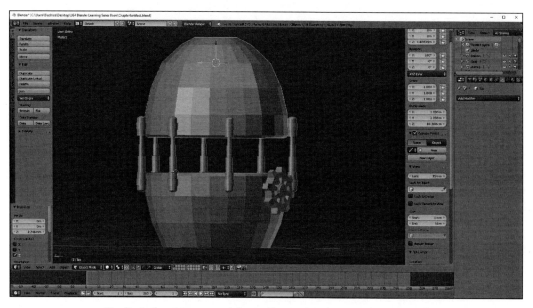

Duplicate the piston around the Artifact so that there are seven in total

8. With the piston pieces all completed, grab your finished piston and **Duplicate** it around the Artifact at equal intervals, similar to what is in the image.

That's it for the pistons! There is only one major set of pieces left to complete and in my opinion they are the most fun: the tentacles! The design calls for the tentacles to be used as handles and legs to give the Artifact an otherworldly feel. To make these weird creations, we will use a combination of a **Bezier Curve** and some modifiers to copy a section of tentacle along a path. This also has the added bonus of making them flexible and easily posed.

On to the next step! The tentacle begins with a basic cube:

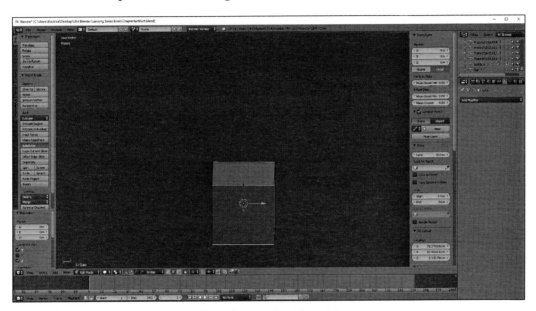

Begin the tentacle with a cube

It's tentacle time! Let's finish the last piece of our creation:

1. Start the tentacle by creating a **Cube** with a 5 cm **Radius**; I know it's not a cylinder but bear with me. Select the four lines through the center of the cube and click **Subdivide** to cut the cube in half.

2. Select all the polygons on the right side of the cube and delete them. Now add the **Mirror** modifier by clicking the wrench icon in the **Properties** pane to open up the **Modifier** menu. Click on the **Add Modifier** dropdown and select **Mirror**. Unlike in *Chapter 2, Starting Our First Project*, we are going to leave this on for the moment before we apply it:

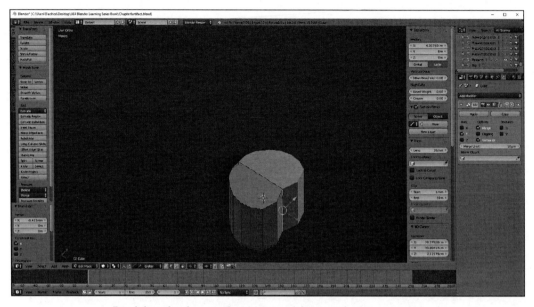

Bevel the cube, then use the Mirror modifier to make it symmetrical

3. Now we are going to make our tentacle by beveling the corners of our cube. Use the **Bevel** tool to apply some rounding to the individual corners until it looks more organic. Yours may look a bit different than mine and that's ok! I used about eight to ten bevels.

4. Time to apply the **Mirror** modifier. Head back to Object mode and click **Apply**:

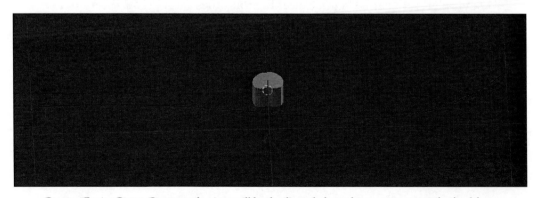

Create a Bezier Curve. Our tentacle piece will be duplicated along the curve to create the final form

5. **Bezier Curves** are curves that have handles which can be moved around to create graceful bends and curves. This provides structure for our tentacle. Head over to **Object** mode and use the **Add** menu, select **Curves**, and choose **Bezier**. Use the **Move** and **Rotate** tools to move it alongside your tentacle piece.

6. All the rest of the fun is in the **Modifiers** menu. On the tentacle object, add an **Array** modifier. Array allows us to create multiple copies of an object, usually in a shape or line. In this case, we will use it to create more tentacle sections along the **Bezier Curve**. In the modifier, change the **Fit Type** to **Fit Curve** and choose the **Bezier Curve** in the next box. Also click the checkbox next to **Merge** and **First Last**; this will improve our result. If your tentacle pieces copy in a weird direction like mine did, change the **X**, **Y**, **Z** numbers under **Relative Offset** until you get the result you want.

7. To finish the tentacle, add a **Curve** modifier. In the **Object** portion of its settings, choose our **Bezier Curve**. The tentacle is now complete! Click on the **Bezier Curve** and head to **Edit** mode. Stretch the two points and see that the tentacle grows as you move them. In the **Scene Properties** panel, changing the **Radius** option under **Transform** can taper the end of your tentacle. Lastly, if you need more control over your tentacle, select the two points on the **Bezier Curve** and click **Subdivide**. This will add another point that can be moved around to better bend and curve your shape:

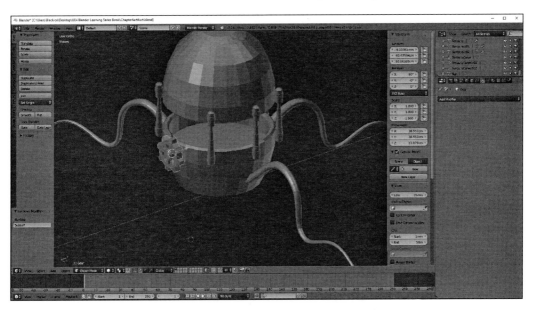

Duplicate the finished tentacle to give the Artifact legs!

8. Finally, use your tentacles to create the legs of the Artifact. Move the first **Bezier Curve** point into contact with our bottom piece. Then move the other points into the shape you want. I used four points per curve. Remember, to duplicate a tentacle you need to copy both the tentacle piece and the **Bezier Curve**.

How is it looking? If you are having problems adjusting the **Bezier Curve** points don't give up! They can be hard to work with at first but the results are worth all the trouble:

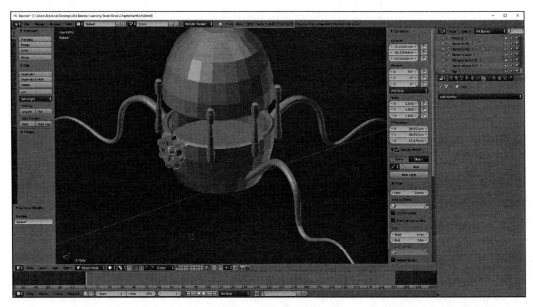

The Artifact has over 7,000 tris!

As we put these great touches on our game asset, there are a couple of things we need to keep track of; luckily Blender does it for us. At the top of the 3D viewport, Blender keeps a count of the total number of **Faces** (polygons) and **Tris** our asset has. This is important because game engines have to work harder to display our level the more **Tris** our assets have. Currently, the Tri limit in Unreal for a single static mesh is 10,000, and that would be a character or weapon, something the player looks at closely. Some of our pieces have pretty high tri counts. In the next chapter, we will take a look at ways to optimize each piece of the Artifact before we UV Unwrap it.

Summary

In this chapter, we went through the art process for designing and producing a complex game asset with a specific narrative and background in mind. The result is the Artifact, an eldritch terror weapon created by followers of a forgotten god. This game asset uses multiple shapes and was designed with function and animation in mind. As part of its design, we built gears and pistons, as well as some otherworldly tentacles. This thing is most assuredly responsible for the disappearance of both the crew of the cargo ship and the inhabitants of our space station. In the next chapter, we will take a look at what it takes to UV Unwrap something this complex, as we prep our game asset for animation and get it ready for Unreal.

7

Let's Dress to Impress!

The Artifact is ready to unleash its hellish power! However, it doesn't really look like much with its default grey exterior. Just like we did in *Chapter 3, It's Time to Customize!* we need to UV Unwrap it so that we can create a material for it and bring it into Unreal. Unlike our crate, the Artifact is a much more complex object and is made of multiple smaller objects. This will require us to use a different technique to create the UV map and for that we need some different tools. Rather than use the Smart UV Project option, we will use custom seams to flatten out the different sections of the Artifact. In this chapter, we will cover the following topics:

- Unwrapping complex objects
- Custom seams and the Unwrap tool
- Using Smart UV Project along with other mapping tools
- Using different types of texture maps together, to create a more realistic look

Unwrapping complex objects

Back in *Chapter 3, It's Time to Customize!*, we learned a simple technique for UV unwrapping called Smart UV Project, a tool that can unwrap simple objects automatically. This process worked great for our crate, but the crate was little more than a slightly modified box. The crate really didn't have much in the way of curves and its triangle count only reached 516. The Artifact will take a little bit more work to unwrap. Our new asset contains 42 separate pieces and has a whopping 54,000 triangles. To unwrap this monstrous game asset, we will need to apply several new tools and techniques.

Marking seams

Seams are lines along which **Unwrap** tool can slice an object to flatten it out during the unwrapping process:

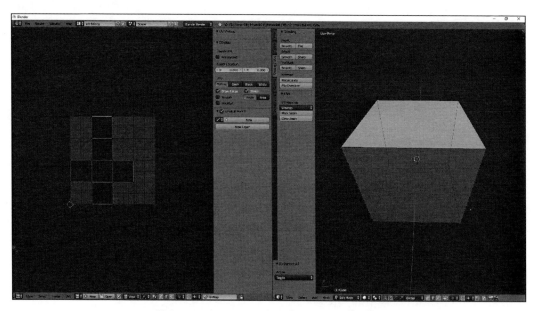

Using custom seams to UV Unwrap a basic cube

Using the **Mark Seam** tool, we can control which lines becomes seams, giving us complete control of the process. We can also use this tool to hide our seams in places a player will not be able to see them. This can be along areas that are normally hidden, along sharp angles or creases, and in areas where the material we are using changes dramatically.

Unwrap tool

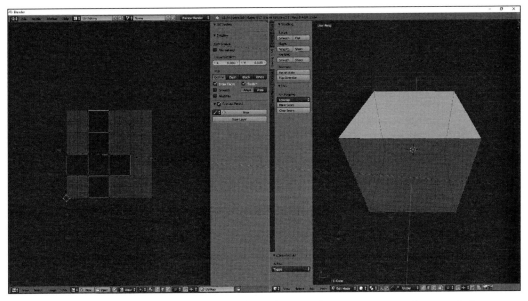

Unwrap tells Blender to mash our object flat, splitting at the custom seams we have marked

After making our seams, we need to tell Blender to flatten out our object. This is done using the **Angle Based Unwrap** tool, or simply the **Unwrap** tool. **Unwrap** takes our seams and treats them like cuts in a cardboard box, then mashes our object flat. The results aren't always perfect. However, Blender has several other tools that can fix these minor issues.

Stitch

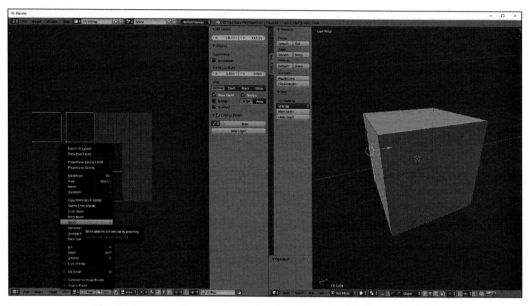

Stitch allows us to fix some errors that the Unwrap tool may have created

Sometimes when marking seams and using the **Unwrap** tool, we may wish to reconnect a couple of faces in our UV map, such as when a seam looks obvious after we place a material on an object and we would like to move it. The **Stitch** tool can be found in the UV menu of the **UV Unwrap** window. Using it is a two-step process. After moving two UV islands (a collection of faces that are connected together in a UV map) that have a shared edge close to each other, we can check whether two faces have shared edges by clicking on an edge in the UV map and looking to see where another orange highlight appears. If you click one edge, another highlights as well; those two edges can be stitched. After lining up the edges, head to the UV menu and select **Stitch**, or press the *V* key. Once the tool is on, we have a few options. The *Tab* key changes whether we are stitching in edge mode or vertex mode. The *S* key turns the **Snap** mode on and off. Snapping will snap the UV island that was first selected to the island that was selected second. We can also choose to stitch the islands at their midpoint, by pressing *M* and turning on the **Midpoint** option. Finally, pressing the *I* key will swap which island will move during stitching. Once we have the settings the way we would like, pressing *Enter* will finalize the stitch.

Average Island Scale

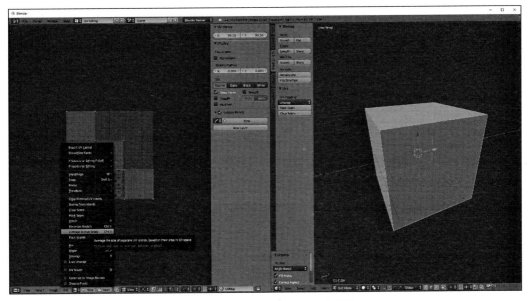

Average Island Scale can be found in the UV menu

Sometimes when unwrapping a complex object, the unwrapping process will create UV islands that are out of scale with the rest of the map. **Average Island Scale** can restore even scaling to UV islands, which will minimize stretching and blurring across the textured area. Simply select the UV islands you wish to average, select the UVs menu at the bottom of the **UV Unwrap** window, and select **Average Island Scaling** or press *Ctrl + A*.

Pack Islands

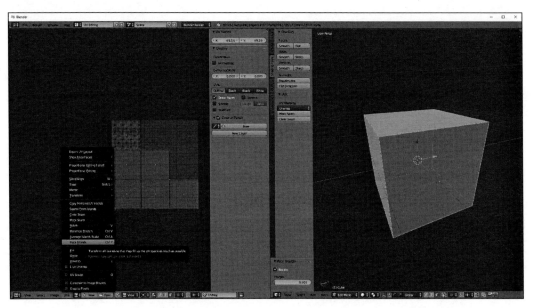

Pack Islands will attempt to arrange and scale your UV islands to achieve the best results

Once we have arranged all of our UV islands, we can use the **Pack Islands** tool and Blender will automatically arrange and scale them to best fit the UV space. This is a great tool to finalize our UV map and get the most out of Blender's UV space. We will use this at the end of our process to try to achieve the best result.

Using Smart UV Project

Before we get started unwrapping each piece of the Artifact, I would like to mention the Smart UV unwrapper one more time. Remember that we used **Smart UV Project** to give us a basic UV map for our crate back in *Chapter 3, It's Time to Customize!*. This tool is great for basic shapes and still has a place in our process for unwrapping more complex objects:

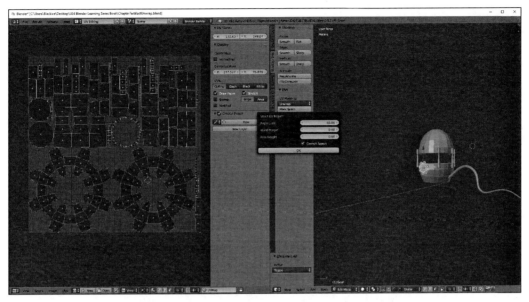

Smart UV Project still has a place inside our expanded toolbox

Since our Artifact contains 42 different pieces, it is likely that **Smart UV Project** will be able to provide us an excellent unwrap solution for some of them. Then, using tools such as **Pack Islands** and **Average Island Scale**, we can add those objects unwrapped with **Smart UV Project** to our overall UV map.

Custom Marking Seams

Let's take a look at using seams effectively. Remember that the **Unwrap** tool will essentially flatten your object for texturing, splitting, and flattening along the lines we have marked as seams. For different primitive shapes such as cubes and cylinders, there are some best practices to be aware of. Knowing these standard unwraps can help us later when we run into more complex shapes, such as our tentacles.

Unwrapping Cubes

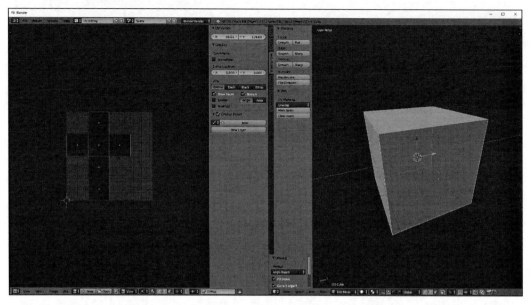

Practice makes perfect! Cubes and other primitive shapes are a great way to brush up on UV unwrapping

When unwrapping a cube, it is important to minimize the number of seams used. This is why we unwrap in a cross shape with the top face at the center. Let's try it!

1. Head up to the **Scene Layout** dropdown and select **UV Editing** from the list.

2. Select the default cube in the scene and head to **Edit** mode. Choose **Line selection** from the selection modes at the bottom of the screen and locate the top face. This will be our reference point as we add our seams.

3. Locate the front face. This can be done by pressing *1* on the number pad or selecting **Front** from the **View** menu. This will be our second point of reference as we unwrap:

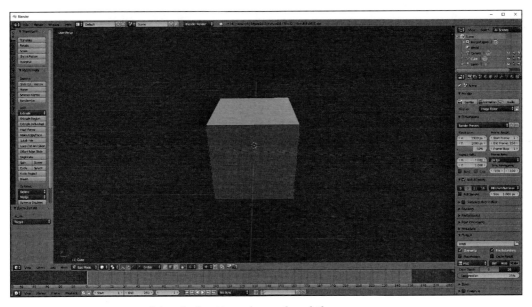

Select the front two edges and mark them as seams

4. Time to create our first seams. Now that we know where our top and front faces are, let's add our first two seams there. Select the two edges shown in the preceding screenshot, click on the **Shading / UVs** tab in the **Tools** panel, and click on the **Mark Seams** button. This will turn the lines red.

5. Now mark the other two vertical edges on the back face. This will create the cross layout we want.

6. Lastly, we want to detach the bottom face from all the other faces except the front. Select the three edges that connect the bottom face to the side and back faces. Mark those as seams.

7. Let's **Unwrap!** Click on the face selection mode and press *A* to select all of the cube's faces. Now press the *U* key and select **Unwrap** from the menu. Your UV map should look like our unwrapped cube.

Turning on the **Stretch** option in our **UV Layout** view will shade the selected objects' UV islands blue, making them easier to see. Turning on **Keep UV and Edit mode mesh selections in sync** will help as well.

Unwrapping Cylinders

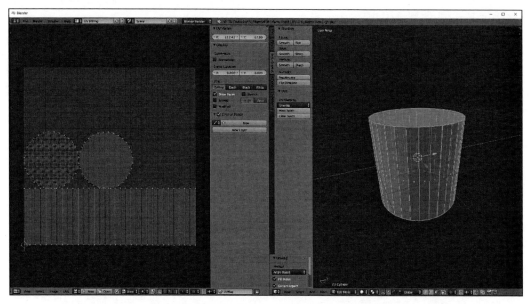

An unwrapped cylinder. Many of the Artefact's 42 shapes will be similar to this

Unwrapping a cylinder is even easier than unwrapping a cube. To unwrap this type of primitive shape, create your seams all the way around the top and bottom faces and then one seam that runs from top to bottom. Try it out and see if your results are similar to what is shown in the preceding screenshot. It's kind of like putting a label on a soup can.

 Want more practice UV unwrapping? It can be good practice to learn to unwrap all the primitives Blender has in the Mesh portion of the **Add** menu!

Once we have a good handle on unwrapping basic primitives, it's time to start tackling the Artifact, piece by piece!

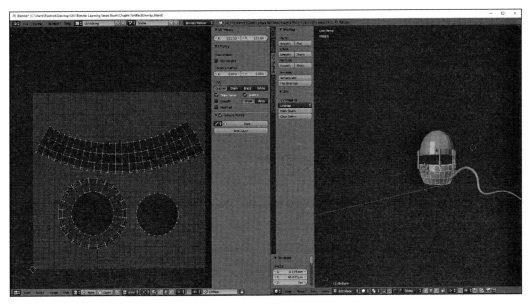

Results of unwrapping the bottom

Let's get started with the bottom portion:

1. In **Object** mode, select the bottom portion of the Artifact and press *Shift + H*. This will isolate our selection by hiding everything that is not selected. Next, head up to the **Scene Layout** drop-down box and select **UV Layout**. This will split your screen into two large viewports: one for manipulating your object and another for working with your UV map:

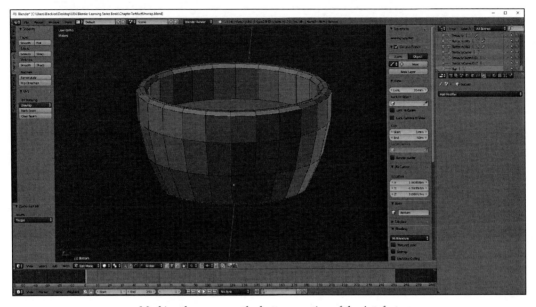

Marking the seams on the bottom portion of the Artefact

 You can isolate a piece of your model by selecting it in **Object** mode and pressing *Shift + H*. To make everything visible again, use *Alt + H*.

2. Time to cut some seams. Unwrapping this part of our creation is not unlike unwrapping a cylinder. Let's first create the seam to detach the inside. Select the top edge loop by selecting **Line** mode, click the first line of the edge loop, hold the *Alt* key, and select the second line of the loop. This will select the entire loop for you. Now head to the tools panel and select the **Shading/UVs** tab. Now click on **Mark Seam**. This will highlight your selected edge loop in red, letting you know that Blender will use this loop as a seam in your UV unwrap.

3. Now repeat the process to select the edge around the bottom face and turn that into a seam as well.

4. Finally, complete the process by selecting edges in a vertical line that runs down from the top marked edge loop to the bottom loop. Mark this as a seam as well, just like we would to unwrap a cylinder.

5. Time to **Unwrap**! Set your **Screen Layout** to **UV Editing**. Now turn off **Face select** mode and press *A* to select all your faces. Finally, press *U* and select **Unwrap** from the menu. Check out the results and see if they are similar to the UV map shown previously.

And we're done with the bottom! Not too hard is it? We will find that many of the pieces of the Artifact unwrap very similarly to cubes and cylinders. This gives us an easy starting point for each piece, taking the guesswork out of getting started:

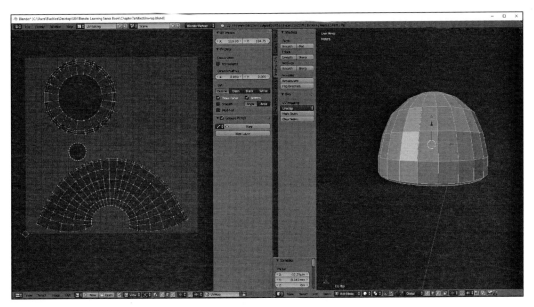

The results of unwrapping the top

The top should be just like the bottom piece:

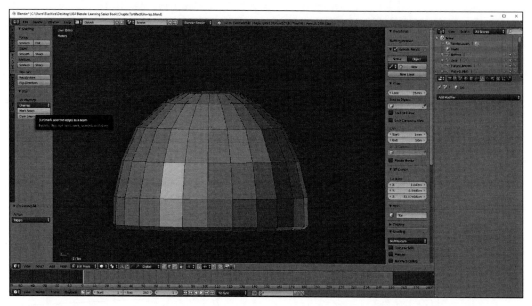

The seams are marked just like the bottom portion and it's similar to unwrapping a cylinder primitive

Let's dive right in:

1. Grab the edge loop around the top polygon and mark that as a seam for the **Unwrap** tool.

2. Select one of the bottom edge loops around where the top and the bottom pieces meet and mark this as a seam as well.

3. Create a vertical seam to connect the other two seams, similar to what we did for the bottom piece.

4. Finally, select all of the faces and use the **Unwrap** tool again. The result should be very similar to what we have for the bottom.

Now that we have the top and the bottom pieces unwrapped, let's switch gears and take a look at the gear (switch gears, get it?):

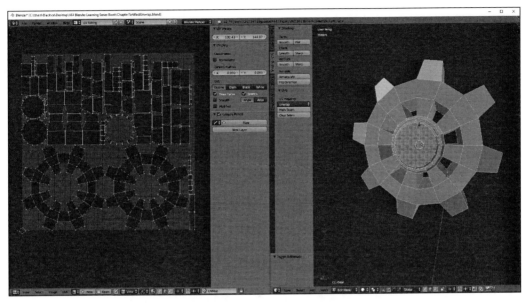

We will use Smart UV Project to unwrap the gear section

For this piece, we are going to use **Smart UV Project**.

1. In **Object** mode, select the gear and head into **Edit** mode. Make sure your selection mode is set to **Face** select and then press *A* to select all of our faces.

2. Press *U* to open the **Unwrap** menu and select **Smart UV Project**. Your results should look similar to the preceding screenshot.

This leaves us only two sets of objects left, the pistons and the tentacles. The processes for both will be similar. We will delete all but one and UV map it. When we copy the mapped section again to replace the deleted pieces, they will keep all of our UV mapping. Now that's working smart!

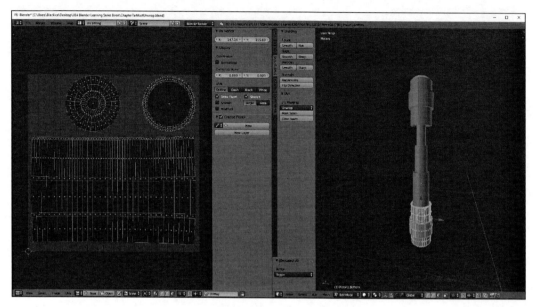

Unwrapping the bottom portion of the piston

Now to take a look at the Piston:

1. Choose which set of piston parts you wish to unwrap and delete all the others. We will be replacing them shortly:

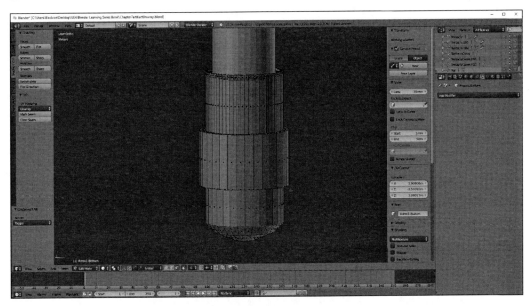

Unwraps just like a cylinder!

2. Start with the bottom piece of the piston. The UV map for this will be similar to a cylinder. Starting at the top, select the top edge loop where the sides and the top meet and mark that as a seam.

3. Next, select the edge loop right before the bottom starts to curve away from the side, and mark that a seam.

4. Finally, open the **Unwrap** menu and select **Unwrap**!

5. Now, delete the top part of the piston and copy the bottom, since the top is just a duplicate of the bottom.

6. This next part covers a few steps. For each of the smaller middle sections, they are simply cylinders and unwrap using the method we spoke of earlier in the chapter. Unwrap all three cylinder sections:

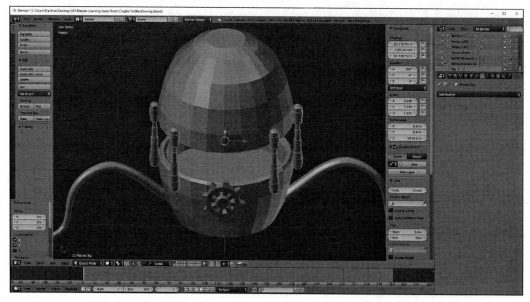

Duplicating the piston parts, just like we did before

7. With all of the parts unwrapped, select all of the piston parts in **Object** mode and duplicate them to replace the pistons we deleted. Congratulations! We have now unwrapped seven pistons!

Lastly, let's take a look at what it will take to unwrap the tentacle:

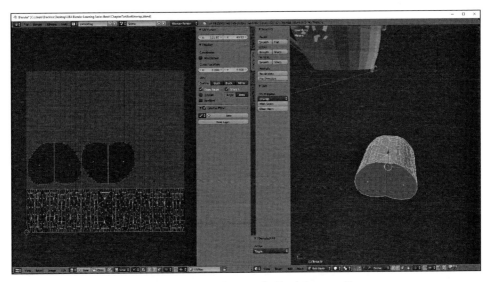

The unwrap for the tentacle. Don't be scared!

Although it may look complicated, it is not much different than a cylinder. However, there is a bit of prep we have to do before we unwrap it:

1. Select one tentacle piece and delete the others. We will unwrap one and copy it:

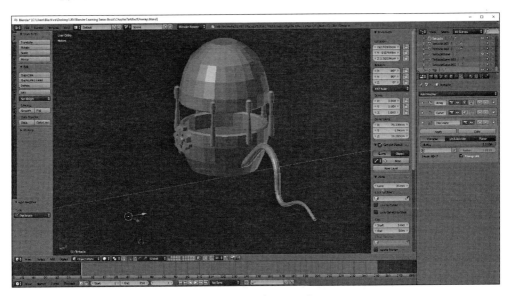

Delete every tentacle except for one

2. We are going to use the **Decimate** modifier to reduce the triangle count on our tentacles. Select the **Modifier** menu (the small wrench) over in the Properties pane. Click on the **Add Modifier** dropdown and choose **Decimate** from the options. In the Decimate modifier itself, turn on the **Triangulate** option. UE4 will triangulate it anyway, so why not have **Decimate** get a head start. The goal of using **Decimate** is to find a ratio that lowers the number of tris that are part of an object, while still maintaining its overall shape. Now, click and slide on the **Ratio** option. We are going to **Decimate** our tentacle by lowering the ratio to somewhere between .70 and .80. This will remove about 20-30% of the triangles and make the entire tentacle more manageable for UE4. Once you have found a Ratio that looks good, click on **Apply**:

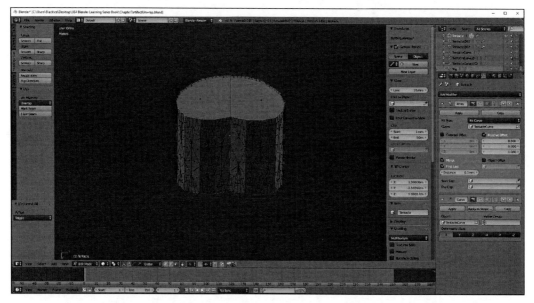

Marking the seams on the tentacle. Again, it is very similar to a cylinder.

3. Surprisingly, unwrapping our tentacle is not unlike unwrapping a cylinder, and we will treat it roughly the same way. First, turn off the modifiers we placed on the tentacle by clicking on the eye icon on each of the modifiers in the **Modifier** menu. Then, select the edge loops around the top and bottom polygons and make them seams. Finally, create a vertical seam to connect these two seams, press *U* to bring up the **Unwrap** menu, and select **Unwrap**.

Each of our pieces is now unwrapped and ready to go! Back in *Chapter 3, It's Time to Customize!* we exported our shape out of Blender as a .FBX file and then brought it into Unreal. This time, we are going to take a look at the different types of texture map that go into making a top notch material and create something spectacular using Allegorithmic's Substance Painter.

Using different maps to create a more realistic look

Materials in Unreal Engine 4 are made of several different textures working together to provide a realistic result. Generally, a material for a game asset has at least two to three different texture maps that are being manipulated by different mathematical nodes. These maps are usually a **Diffuse map**, a **Specular map**, and a **Normal map**:

The coloring of the Artifact is determined by the Diffuse map

Diffuse maps are the basic colors that we have painted on our objects. Unreal accepts these textures in the **Material Editor** as the object's **Base Color**. These maps generally contain color and pattern information that is painted directly onto a copy of the object's UVs in programs such as Photoshop. Simply put, this type of map contains the surface colors of our object.

Next is the Specular map:

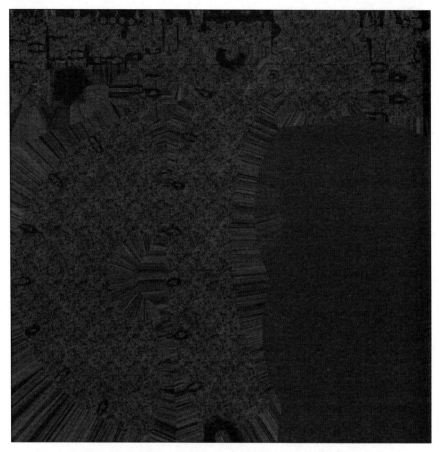

The Specular map controls how light behaves when it hits a surface

Specular maps control how shiny or dull a surface appears to be and can be hand painted or exported out of different programs, such as Autodesk Mudbox. These maps are a great way to make parts of an object appear as if they have been shined or cleaned. When looking at a specular map, the lighter areas of the map are where players will see a shiny surface, whereas the darker areas of the map will appear dulled.

Finally, there is the normal map:

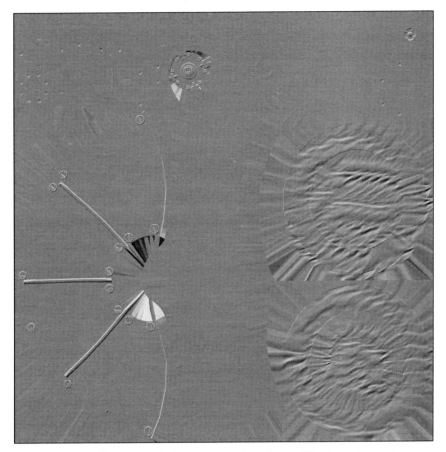

The normal map can help fake some details without adding to our tri count

Normal maps store detailed information from high polygon versions of game assets that can then be used to create detail on lower polygon versions of those same game assets. This detailed information is stored in three colors, red, green, and blue, and each color corresponds to a different axis in 3D space. The information is then used to simulate depth and can make a game asset look much more detailed than it actually is.

These days, there are many different ways to generate these types of texture map. Diffuse and Specular maps can be painted onto copies of a game asset's UVs using programs such as Photoshop and GIMP. Normal maps usually need to be created with a separate program, such as the freely available Xnormal. However, there is another type of texturing that is quickly gaining popularity. The process is called **Physically Based Rendering (PBR)** and seeks to simulate what light actually does using Diffuse maps, Specular maps, Roughness values, and Metallic values, as opposed to more traditional methods. Where game artists used to be required to guess how light would interact with their game characters and objects, PBR allows them to paint their materials onto their game assets while the computer simulates the lighting. The results tend to be much more accurate and work well in most lighting situations. One of the most popular tools for PBR is Allegorithmic's Substance Painter.

Before we tackle Substance Painter, there is one thing on our model that needs to be fixed. When we used the **Decimate** tool on our tentacle, it may have created some ugly geometry that is not doing our triangle count any favors:

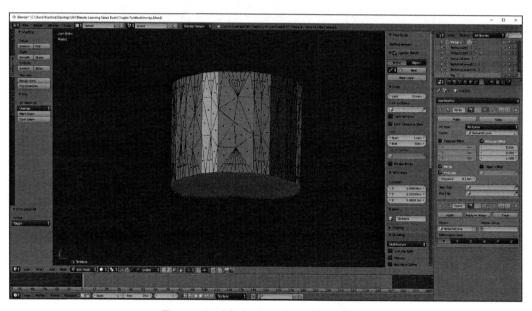

Time to simplify the geometry of the tentacle

There are a lot of lines here that we simply do not need! This process is called Retopologizing, or simply retopoing, and is simply us going back to an object and simplifying the geometry, while still maintaining the original shape. Let's just jump right in:

1. Select our tentacle and press *Shift + H* to isolate it before we head back into **Edit** mode.

2. In the **Modifier** menu of the **Properties** pane, turn off both the **Array** and **Curve** modifiers by clicking on the eye icon in each of their respective menus:

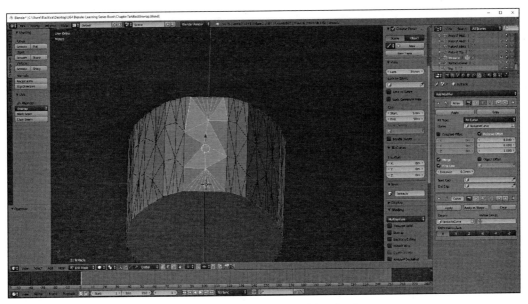

Select many of the inner lines and dissolve them

3. Looking at the geometry, there are several lines we can remove while still keeping the basic shape. Select all the lines similar to the selections shown in the preceding screenshot. Press *X* or the *Delete* key and select **Dissolve** Edges. This will fully remove both the edge and the vertices that go with them:

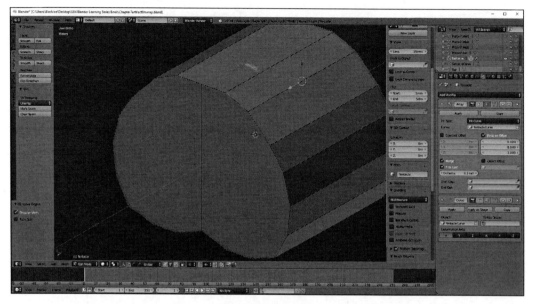

There! All cleaned up.

4. Repeat the process for each major face of the tentacle until we have clear and simple geometry! Don't worry about our UV map. It has been automatically updated with our changes.

5. Lastly, head back to **Object** mode a turn our modifiers back on; we are going to need them. We need to **Apply** both modifiers to the model, but order is important. First apply the **Array** modifier, and then the **Curve** modifier. Finally, we can delete the **Tentacle Curve** that we used as a guide for our shape. It is no longer needed.

Now that we have cleaned that up, let's take a look at using Substance Painter to create an interesting material for the Artifact:

 Substance Painter is available for a 30-day free trial and can be downloaded at `https://www.allegorithmic.com/products/substance-painter`.

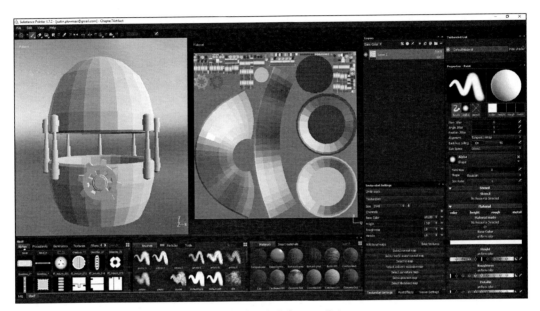

The Artefact inside Substance Painter

Substance Painter will allow us to paint color and detail directly onto the Artifact, and will create all the necessary texture maps we need, based on our result. The process will take a few steps:

1. First, we will tweak our UV maps in Blender to prepare for exporting.

2. Second, we will export an FBX file out of Blender and use it to create a Substance Painter project.

3. Third, we will paint detail onto the Artifact.

4. Fourth, we will add color.

5. Finally, we will export the texture maps out of Substance Painter to use in Unreal 4.

It seems like a long process, but the results are definitely worth the time.

For the Artifact to work with Substance Painter, we need to join all the pieces together and tweak our UV map:

1. Joining all of our objects together is a pretty straightforward process. In the **Scene Outliner**, click on the first piece at the top of the list, then, while holding the *Shift* key, select each of the other pieces in the list, making sure to skip the tentacle. We will texture this piece separately.

2. With all of the objects selected, press *Ctrl + J*. This will join them into one object and will combine all of their UV maps into one.

3. Head up to the **Screen Layout** dropdown and select the **UV Layout** option. Select our new combined Artifact and select all of its faces. Our map will be a jumble where all of our unwraps have begun to overlap:

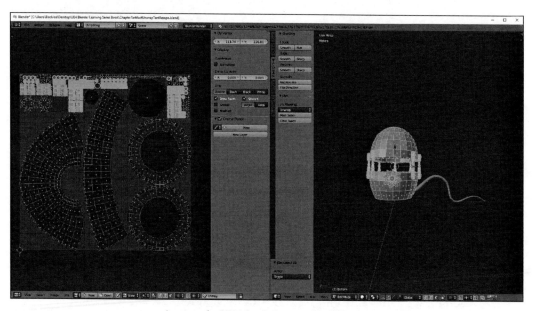

Arrange the UV islands into one big UV map

4. Now head to the **UV** menu and select **Average Island Scale**. This should change the scaling of all of our UV islands relative to each other. Next, select **Pack Islands** from the **UV** menu to pack them all in the one-to-one UV space for us. Our result should look similar to the preceding screenshot:

Set the Smoothing option to Face

Alright, everything is ready for us to export. With the Artifact selected, head to the **File** menu and export an FBX. Make sure to select **Selected Objects** in your **Export FBX** options. Also, head over to the **Geometries** portion of that menu and change the **Smoothing** dropdown to **Face**. Export!

This next section requires the 30-day trial of Substance Painter and the demo files for their Substance Painter Texturing for Beginners course on YouTube. The demo files can be downloaded at `https://s3.amazonaws.com/alg-releases/public_releases/tutorials/scifi_crate/scifiCrate.zip`. I highly recommend this course, as it gives you a great introduction to Substance Painter and Physically Based Rendering.

Time to open Substance Painter! For anybody who has had some experience with Photoshop, the interface has a similar look and feel. Take a few minutes to explore some of the information panes. If you feel they would work better in different places, they can be rearranged exactly like the panes in Unreal. Just grab the one you wish to move and drag it to the new location.

As we move forward, we will not be going over every feature in Substance Painter. I will be highlighting only those we need to complete the Artifact. I highly recommend taking advantage of their free training on YouTube if you would like to know more.

The first thing we need to do is create a project and import our FBX file:

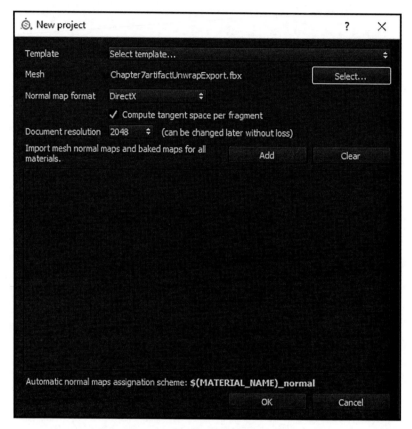

Importing the FBX file into Substance Painter

1. Head to the upper-left corner of the screen and select the **File** menu. Then select **New**. Match your project settings to those in the preceding screenshot. Clicking the **Select** button in the window will allow us to choose our FBX for the project.

2. Now that we have our project set up, go ahead and save it. Much like Unreal Engine 4, Substance Painter is a sophisticated program that uses a significant amount of your computer's resources. This can cause it to become unstable at times and crash. Remember to save often!

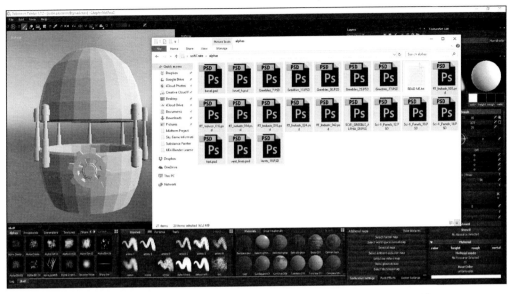

Import all of the PSD files from the Alphas folder of the Sci Fi Crate tutorial

3. Let's import some additional tools into the program. Find where you saved the Sci Fi Crate tutorial assets and unzip the file. In the **Alphas** folder, we will find several new alphas that Substance Painter can use as detail brushes. Select all of the PSD files in the folder and drag them into the **Alphas** tab of the **Shelf** — the large window that runs along the bottom of the screen. That will add them to the project for our use:

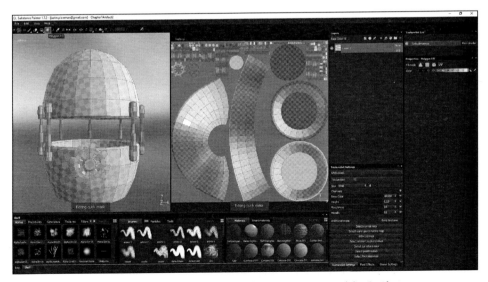

Creating a mask so that we only color in certain parts of the Artifact

4. Time to begin adding details. Substance Painter works by changing the **Height, Color, Roughness**, and **Metallic** properties of an object to add detail and color without adding any new geometry. We will be adding new features to the Artifact, such as corrosion, seams, rivets, and more. These details will be added to a normal map that we can then use in Unreal. To get started, let's mask off the sections we would like to work with first. Press *T* to switch to **Quick Mask** mode. Now click **Polygon Fill** in the menu bar located in the top left of the screen. This will allow us to mask off the sections we want to work with by coloring polygons. Over in the **Properties** pane on the far right, slide the **Color** slider all the way to the left. We want to color in the sections we want to protect in black. Those left white will be edited by the tools we will use:

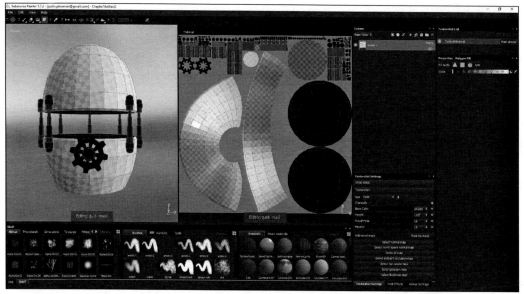

Mask off all but the top and bottom

5. Select the **UV** button in the **Properties** pane. This will allow us to fill whole UV islands. Click the outer shell of both the top and bottom sections of the Artifact. Next, rotate the 3D view by holding *Ctrl* and using the *left mouse button* so that you can select the large polygons located at the top and bottom. If the Artifact slides out of view, use *Ctrl + middle mouse button* to slide the camera. Once you have selected those polygons, Press the *I* key to invert the selection. Now we can add details to the outside without touching any of the other parts. Once we are done with masking, click back on the paintbrush in the menu bar to head back to painting mode, and press *T* to stop editing our **Quick Mask** and begin using it:

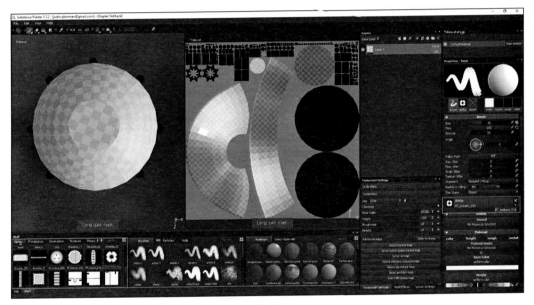

Let's add some details to the very top

6. In the **Alphas** pane, select the **RT_Industr_019** alpha and drag it to the **Alpha** option in the **Properties** pane. Underneath the **Alphas** option in the **Properties** pane is the **Material** section. Click the buttons for **Color**, **Rough**, and **Metal** to turn them off. We only want to affect the **Height** channel with these first details. (If you cannot see the options, click the **Layer 1** layer in the **Layers** pane.) Rotate the camera so that you can see the top polygon of the Artifact. You can look at an exact top view by holding *Alt*, then holding *Shift*, and finally using the *left mouse button* to rotate the view to the top. The view should snap to a top view. Move the cursor to the center of the top polygon, hold *Ctrl + right mouse button*, and drag to resize the tool to fit the face. Over in the **Properties** pane, find the **Height** slider in the **Material** section. This slider controls whether we will have detail that sticks out of the Artifact or cuts into it, by using a value between -1 and 1. -1 will cut grooves into our object just like a cookie cutter. 1 will add detail on top of our object. Slide the slider all the way to the right to give it a value of 1, line up our brush with the top, and click. If you don't like the result, undo it and try again:

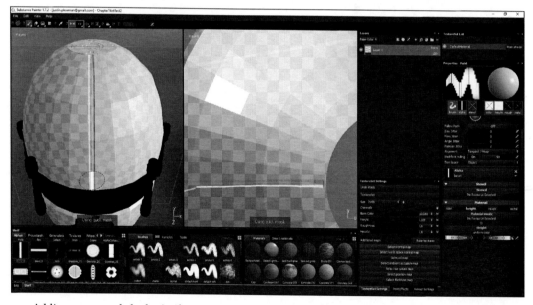

Adding seams can help the Artifact seem more real. The Symmetry tool can cut your work time in half.

7. To save us some time, we are going to turn on the **Symmetry** option in the toolbar. Turn on **Symmetry** and adjust the **Mirror** axis with the button to the right. Here, I am using **Mirror Z**.

8. Back in the **Alphas** pane, select the **Bevel** alpha and drag it into the **Properties** pane. This alpha creates seams similar to where two metal plates fit together. Next, slide the **Height** slider into the negative range. I slid mine all the way to the left for `-1`. Adjust the size of the tool to something a bit smaller using *Ctrl + right mouse button*, and click the *left mouse button* once to start our seam. Holding the *Shift* key allows us to create a straight line from the last place we clicked. Hold *Shift* and stretch the dotted line until the brush meets our top detail. Clicking the *left mouse button* will now create a straight seam from where we started to the top of the object. Since we are using **Symmetry**, it also creates a seam for us on the back side as well.

9. Now switch our **Mirror** axis back to *X* and create another seam along the sides of the Artifact, similar to what we did on the front and back:

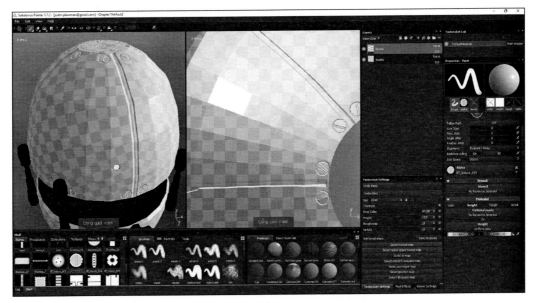

Rivets make the Artifact seem like it is made from metal plates

10. Let's add some rivets! Create a new layer in the **Layers** pane by clicking the **+** button and rename it to Rivets by double-clicking the layer name. We might also want to rename **Layer 1** to **Seams**. Remember that naming is important! Change the alpha we are using to **RT_Industr_010**, resize your brush, and begin placing rivets near the corners of our new "metal plates." Remember to use the **Mirror X** and **Mirror Z** symmetry axis options to make the process easier.

11. Add as many rivets and seams as you want to the top and bottom sections of the Artifact to personalize it and make it your own. Just remember to use a new layer each time you want to create a new group of details.

12. Now press *T* to go back to editing the **Quick Mask** and press *I* to invert the mask again. Now add detail to the **Gear** and **Pistons**, just like we did for the outer shell of the Artifact.

13. Finally, let's create a folder in our **Layers** pane by clicking the little folder button. Name it Height Info and then drag each of your layers into it. This way, we can keep everything organized.

How is the Artifact looking? Using this amazing tool, we've been able to add some great detail to what might have been a somewhat boring model. However, we still need to add some color and really make this game asset shine! To simplify the process, we will take advantage of Substance Painter's Smart Materials, collections of preset materials and settings that are perfect for saving us time. When we combine these with a mask, we are able to apply these great looking materials to specific parts of the Artifact.

We will use Smart Materials to give the Artifact a sinister look in just a short time. Let's get started!

1. Click on over to the **Smart Materials** tab and scroll down to the **Steel dark stained** material. Click this material and drag it into the **Layers** pane. This will apply the material to the whole game asset:

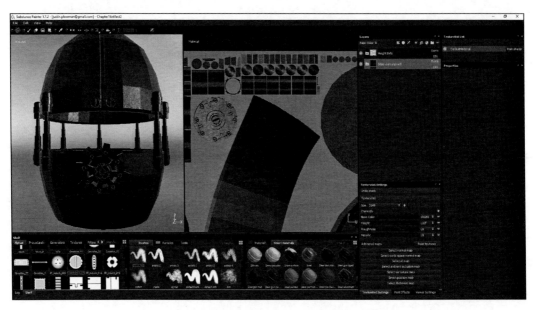

Apply the Steel dark stained material

2. Now find the **Silver Armor** material and drag it into the **Layer** pane. Make sure that it is above **Steel dark stained** in the layer stack.

3. Right-click on **Silver Armor** and select **Add White Mask** from the menu.

4. Back in the toolbar, turn on the **Polygon Fill** tool. Just like we did with the **Quick Mask**, slide the **Color** slider in the **Properties** pane all the way to the left and click the **UV** button. Now select the outside shell of the Artifact on both the top and bottom piece. Also select the bottom polygon. This will allow the steel layer underneath to show through the **Silver Armor** layer. The result is that the gear and pistons are now silver, while the outer shell remains a sinister dark metal:

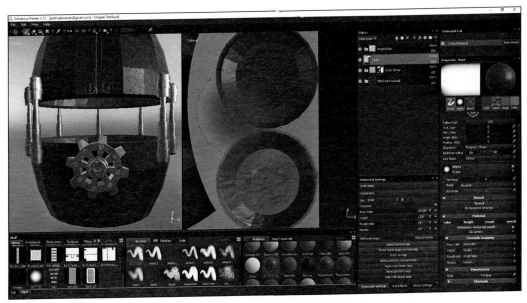

Color the inside of the Artifact using the Satin generic material

5. One more section to go! We are going to add a satin material to the inside of the Artifact. Create a new layer that sits above our Smart Materials in the layer stack and name it Satin. Press *T* to create a **Quick Mask** and mask off everything except the interior of the Artifact. In the **Materials** tab of the **Shelf**, scroll down and select the **Satin Generic** material. Next, set your alpha to **Shape**. Finally, over in the UV layout side of the view, click and drag the brush around the interior faces of the Artifact. This will paint the material directly onto the UV map and works exactly like painting on the model.

And we are done with our materials! Time to get these great-looking texture maps out of Substance Painter and ready for Unreal 4.

1. We start with baking a **Normal** map. Click the **Bake Textures** button over in the **TextureSet Settings** pane. Turn off all of the options except for **Normal**. Leave all the options at their default and click **Bake Textures** down near the bottom of the window. We should now see a normal map added our **Additional Maps** list:

Open the Export Textures menu

2. Next, click on the **File** menu and select **Export Textures**. Click on the **Configurations** tab. This lists several different presets that we can use, based on where our game asset is going next. Although there is an Unreal Engine 4 option, we are going to click the **+** near the top of the window and create our own preset. Double-click the new preset and name it **Normal**.

3. This preset will be created to export our normal map only, without any of the maps we don't need quite yet. In the **Output Maps** section of the window, click the **RGB** button to create an RGB channel for our normal map. Next, click and drag the **Normal DirectX** option from the **Converted Maps** section of the window onto the RGB option, in the new channel we just created. The channel will output our normal map. Finally, give the channel the name **Normal**.

4. Back in the **Export Textures** menu, head back to the **Export** tab. Change the **Config** dropdown to our new **Normals** option and click the **Export** button down at the bottom of the window. After a few seconds, we should receive a message saying that our export has successfully finished. Click the **Open Folder** option to navigate to our new normal map:

Use the Normal map we generated to test whether or not the Artifact has retained our height information

5. Our normal map contains all of our detail information that was stored in our **Height** channel. In **Shelf**, click over to the **Textures** tab. Now bring up the folder that contains our new normal map and drag the map into the **Textures** tab. Finally, click the **Normal Map** over in the **Additional Maps** section of the **TextureSet Settings** pane and select our new normal map from the options. We can test it out by heading to the **Layers** pane and turning off our **Height Info** folder. If all of our details remain, we are all set!

6. Next, head back to the **Bake Textures** menu and turn off all of the options except for **Ambient Occlusion**. This type of map enhances the shadows in the nooks and crannies of our game asset and can be utilized by Unreal 4.

7. Time for one final export. Head to the **File** menu and select **Export Textures** again. From the menu, select **Unreal Engine 4 (Packed)**. Lastly, click the **Export** button!

And we are finally done texturing this thing! Now that you have a good feel for how Substance Painter works, I would encourage you to run through the process again for our tentacle. Substance Painter has some interesting options for realistic skin that just might be perfect for bringing a weird and creepy feel to this part of our asset.

Summary

Wow, what a ride! In this chapter we explored different UV unwrapping techniques and applied them to the different portions of the Artifact. We then joined all of the different pieces of our game asset together and created one unified UV map. With our UV map in hand, we imported the Artifact into Substance Painter, a texturing program that utilizes Physically Based Rendering techniques to create realistic material solutions. Within this sophisticated program, we painted new detail directly onto the Artifact pieces and splashed an amazing coat of paint on them to enhance the Artifact's sinister look. In the next chapter, we will explore ways to animate the Artifact and assemble the final version of this sinister object in Unreal Engine 4.

8
Lights, Camera, Animation!

The Artifact has come a long way. What started out as an idea on a piece of drawing paper has become a full 3D model, complete with textures. However, we are not finished bringing this forgotten relic to full hellish life. If you will recall in the original design for this game asset, the Artifact has to be able to open at the touch of the player, making them an unwitting accomplice to its destructive purpose. For that, we need animation! Blender has a complete suite of animation tools that is more than up to the task. Using keyframes, we will create a simple open animation and prepare the Artifact for export into our space station level. In this chapter, we will cover the following topics:

- How does Blender handle animation?
- Rigging and using keyframes
- Using Blender's suite of animation tools

How does Blender handle animation?

You might remember back in *Chapter 2, Starting Our First Project*, that we touched very briefly on keyframes, those little recorded points in time that we use to animate objects. Blender uses tools that are very similar to using **Timeline** and **Matinee** in UE4, so let's spend a little bit of time building on that knowledge. Remember that keyframes represent important positions in time in our animations. In the case of our door, it was the open and closed positions. For our elevator, it was the up and down positions.

Those keyframes help Unreal and Blender to create what are called **Tweens** — all those little minor movements in between major points. Along with the keyframes, 30 of them make up one second of animation. Back in the heyday of Bugs Bunny, Road Runner, and the Flintstones, animation houses had Senior Animators, who would create all the keyframes. They would then turn those over to Junior Animators who would draw all of the tween frames by hand. This process used to be very long and labor intensive. Now that we have computers to calculate all the in-between frames for us, the process can be done quite easily.

So what can a keyframe record?

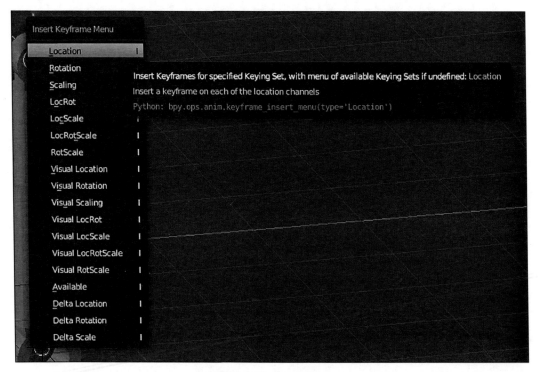

The Insert Keyframes Menu

At first glance, the **Insert Keyframe Menu** gives us several options. However, upon closer inspection, we can see that all of the options are variations on the same three things: **Location**, **Rotation**, and **Scale**. **Location** will be the option that we will use the most, to record the locations of our various piston pieces as they move the lid of the Artifact. We will also use **Rotation** to rotate our gear as part of the locking mechanism.

There is one more technique we can use during our animation that can make our lives a lot easier. A Dummy object, or what Blender calls an **Empty**, is a simple object that is not counted as part of the scene when we export, but can be a huge help when animating. Think of them like the strings on a puppet. Nobody is going to see them, but they will make controlling our animation much easier.

Let's look at the **Empty** menu:

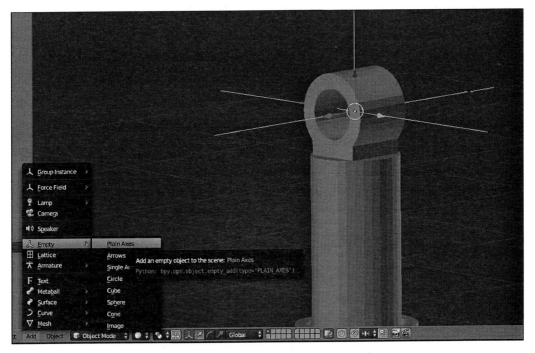

An Empty can be used to make animation easier

Empty objects come in a variety of shapes, from the simple axis shown in the previous picture, to arrows, spheres, and even cones. Objects in the scene we wish to animate can be linked to these objects so that we only have to move the Empty, essentially creating a handle. They can also be used as a target for an animation constraint.

Rigging and using keyframes

Now that we have a good idea what tools we will need, let's talk about creating keyframes!

The Timeline is used to add keyframes in a similar fashion to Timelines in Unreal 4

Similar to Unreal 4, the keyframes we create will be displayed in the **Timeline**. This area is located directly under the 3D viewport. Keyframes are represented as simple yellow lines, and the amount of time we are viewing can be adjusted by using the mouse wheel.

Now let's start with a basic cube and create some keyframes:

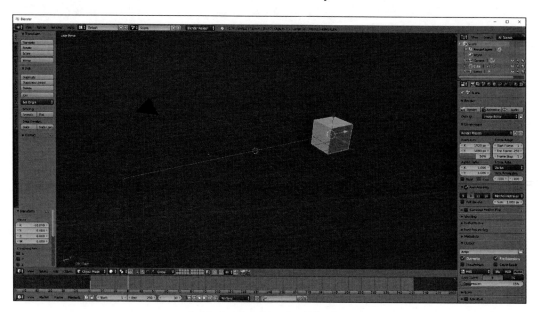

A simple animation of a sliding box

To make a simple animation where our cube moves, we need to create two keyframes:

1. Create the first keyframe by selecting the cube, pressing *I* to open the **Insert Keyframe Menu**, and selecting **Location** at the top of the list.

2. Now slide the time slider in the **Timeline** window to frame 30. This can be done by right clicking on the **Timeline** near 30 and then holding the button to slide it along the **Timeline**. The box highlighted in the image shows the active frame.

3. Next, in the 3D viewport, slide your cube in any direction you like. Finally, press *I* and select **Location** from the menu, just like we did for the first keyframe.

4. Test your animation by clicking and holding the right mouse button on the **Timeline** and sliding the active frame between 1 and 30. We should see the cube slide between our two recorded positions.

Congratulations, we just animated our cube! Now let's take a look at how to change or delete any keyframes that might have been off a bit:

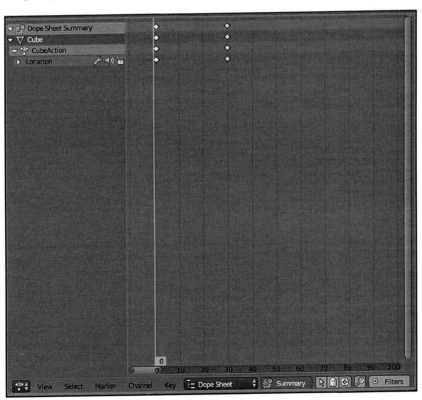

Introducing the Dope Sheet

Sometimes when we are creating our keyframes, we might put one down where we didn't mean to, or we might need to adjust the timing of our animation to feel more natural. The **Dope Sheet** (highlighted in the previous screenshot) allows us to move, copy, and delete our keyframes with relatively simple controls.

To move keyframes, select the keyframes you wish to move. Then click and drag the keyframes to their new time position. Finally, click on the *LMB* again to finalize the new time position.

Here we can see the **Dope Sheet** in action:

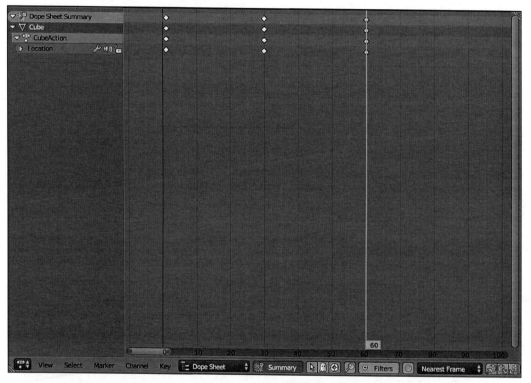

Duplicating keyframes is useful when an animation has to end in the exact place it began

To copy a keyframe, select the keyframe you wish to copy and press *Ctrl + C*. Now right-click and drag the time slider to the new desired time. Finally, press *Ctrl + V* to copy the keyframes. This is a great technique for creating spinning or other cyclical animations where the object has to end exactly where it began.

Time to apply what we know to our Artifact.

To animate our piece, we will need to break it down into a few different pieces. Basically, if it moves, it has to be its own separate piece. Now you might be saying to yourself, *Wait. Then why did we make it all one piece earlier?* For the purposes of UV unwrapping, we had to have the Artifact as one piece. As we separate pieces from the whole, they are still part of the UV map that we made. When we bring the whole thing into Unreal, the material we create will still apply all those great textures to every piece of the Artifact.

Let's start by separating the top section:

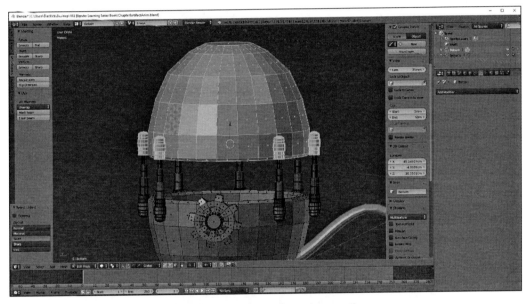

Select the top section and top piston section

This first piece will contain the lid and the tops of the pistons:

1. Select a face on the outside of the lid and press *L*; this should select all the faces that make up the outside of the lid.

2. Next, select a face on the inside of the lid while holding the *Shift* key. This will add the face to our current selection set. Press *L* to select all the faces on the inside of the lid.

3. Now select the very top face.

Now we will add the pistons to the selection:

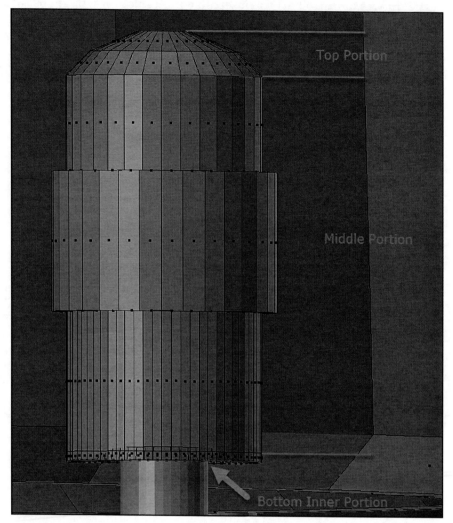

A breakdown of a piston. This will be needed to bind the right parts to the right bones

4. Finally, holding *Shift*, select a polygon on one of the piston's top sections and press *L*. Each piston top is made up of three different sections: the top portion, the middle portion, and the bottom inner portion. Make sure to *Shift* select a face in each section and press *L* to select all the faces in that section.

5. Press *P* to open up the **Separation** menu and select **Selection**. This will separate off the faces we selected to become a new piece. Remember to rename it in the **Scene Outliner** to something you will remember, such as Top.

Now we have our top section separated. Repeat the process for the bottom and the gear. If you select a face, press *L*, and nothing happens, just select the face next to it and try again. Also, pressing *Z* will turn on wireframe mode. This will allow you to select faces through your object. Be sure to select those faces by clicking on the little black dot located at the center of the face.

Time to tackle those middle piston parts! Our plan of attack will have us separate them into three layers, since we will be moving all of them together for the animation. The bottom set of bits will be one layer, the middle set will be another, and so on:

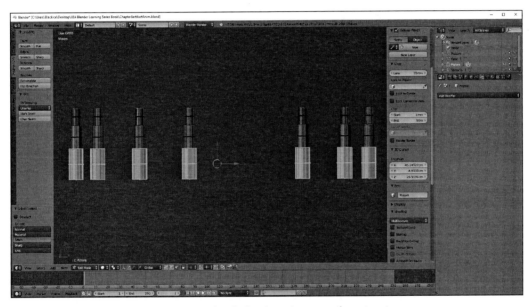

It is necessary to break the piston into parts for animation

 Remember that you can use *Shift + H* in **Object** mode to hide everything that isn't what you have selected!

Here is how we do it:

1. Select your piston parts and use *Shift + H* to hide the rest of the Artifact.

2. Head to **Edit** mode and select the bottom portion of each piston set, just like in the previous screenshot.

3. Press *P* and choose **Selection** from the menu. Rename the layer `Pistons.Bottom` in the **Scene Outliner**.

4. Hide them by clicking on the eye next to their name in the **Scene Outliner**. This will make the rest of the process much easier.

5. Repeat this process for the middle layer. This will leave the top layer separated for you.

If everything went well, your **Scene Outliner** should look something like this:

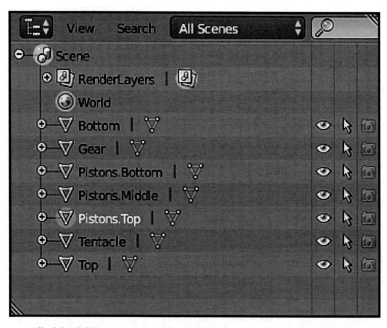

All of the different sections of the Artifact that we will use for animation

With everything separated out, there is one more step that we need to take before we start animating. Because we are creating a static mesh that includes animations, the Artifact will be brought into Unreal as a **skeletal mesh**. Skeletal meshes are created from two parts, the static mesh object itself and a system of bones for manipulating the mesh. That means the Artifact needs bones!

To animate the Artifact, each piece that moves needs a bone. These bones will be connected to a single bone that Unreal will read as the root. We will then animate the bones, rather than the mesh itself.

We will begin with a single bone:

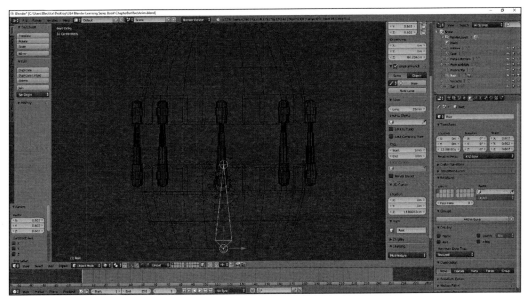

Adding the first bone

Here's how we add it:

1. First, we need to move the 3D cursor to the center of the bottom section. Select the bottom of the Artifact and press *Shift + S* to open the **Snap** menu. Select **Cursor to Selected** to move the 3D cursor into position.

2. Now head to the **Add** menu, select **Armature**, and add in a **Single Bone**. Blender should add it right at the bottom center of the piece. Scale the bone so it lines up with only the bottom section of the Artifact, similar to what you see in the previous screenshot. It might help to press the Z key and look at things in wireframe mode.

3. Select the new bone and head to **Edit** mode:

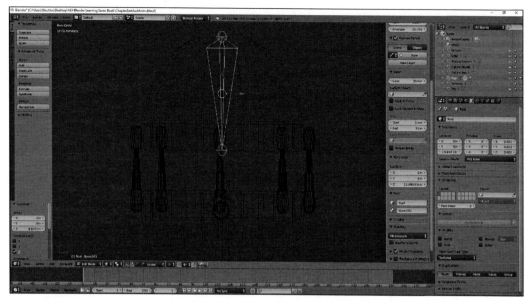

Adding the bone that controls the top

4. Now that we are in **Edit** mode, any bones that we add to the **Armature** for the Artifact will be connected to the first bone as far as Unreal is concerned. This is important, since Unreal only allows one armature per skeletal mesh. Click on the **Add** menu and select **Single Bone**. This will add a new bone to the scene. Using the move arrows, drag the new bone up in the Z-axis to give it some height.

5. Click on the center of the new bone to highlight it and move it into position within the top portion of the Artifact. This bone will control moving the lid up and down during opening. Try to line it up similar to what you see in the image. Since we moved our 3D cursor to the center of the Artifact, all of our bones should be perfectly centered. This will be important when we animate:

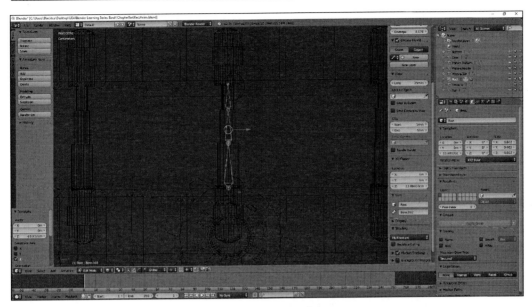

These three bones will control the pistons

6. Time to add three bones to control the piston parts. Just as we did to create the last bone, create a bone to control each layer of the piston. Remember to size them similar to the pieces they control, and line them up as shown in the screenshots:

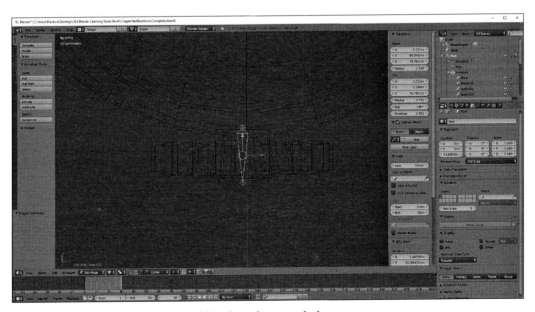

Add the bone that controls the gear

7. One last bone! Create a small bone to control the gear. Once it has been created, move it into position and then rotate it 90 degrees so that it is lying flat. This bone will spin to create the rotating effect for the gear.

With all the bones created, we now have to connect them to each section of the Artifact, so that moving the bones will move the pieces they are tied to. In Blender, this process is called **Parenting**. We will also be checking out a new mode that is exclusive to using Armatures: the **Pose Mode**!

To get to **Pose Mode**, select your Armature and head down to your modes dropdown:

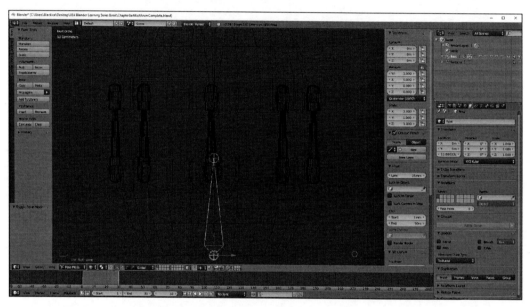

Enter Pose mode by selecting a bone and selecting Pose Mode from the Mode dropdown

From there, select **Pose Mode**. In this mode, we can parent parts of our 3D model to our new bones, and then keyframe them to create our animation of the Artifact opening:

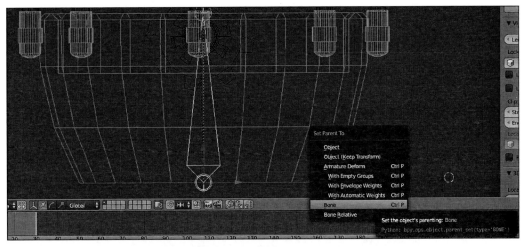

Press Ctrl + P to open the Set Parenting To menu and then choose Bone.
This will bind the bottom section to its appropriate bone

Blender makes the **Parenting** process quick and easy:

1. Select the piece we would like to parent. Let's start with the bottom section.

2. Holding the *Shift* key, select the bone you would like to parent to the bottom of the Artifact. In this case, this is the first bone we created.

3. Press *Ctrl* + *P*; this will open the **Set Parenting To** menu. Select the **Bone** option.

4. Lastly, test that the bone is now connected to the bottom piece by selecting the bone and sliding it in any direction. The bottom of the Artifact should slide with it. Press *Ctrl* + *Z* to return it to its original position.

For each bone, repeat the process to parent them to their respective pieces. Once we have completed the **Parenting** process, we are ready to animate!

Using Blender's suite of animation tools

Time to bring the Artifact to life! Good animation can breathe character and vitality into any object. Many beginning animators start with the *12 Basic Principles of Animation* originally written by Disney animators *Ollie Johnston* and *Frank Thomas* and I highly recommend checking them out. What we will be looking at for the Artifact is basic mechanical animation. Our pistons will move and our gear will rotate. However, I would encourage you to read up on the basics and apply what you've learned later on.

Just like we did earlier when we practiced with the cube, we are going to create some keyframes, but in this case, we will be moving the bones we created and not the pieces of the Artifact itself. The result will be a game asset that we can trigger to open within Unreal:

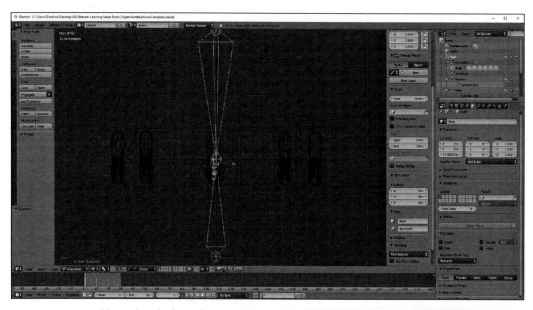

Manipulate the bones by using the Armature group in the Scene Outliner

Using **Pose** mode, let's move the Artifact into the closed position:

1. To make things easier, select your Armature in the **Scene Outliner** and click on the little + icon. This will list all the current features tied to your Armature. Check out the **Pose** option. For each bone that we created, there is a little bone icon that we can click to select and deselect specific bones. This will be very handy as we move forward.

2. Using the **Scene Outliner**, select each bone in turn and move them down until the Artifact is closed. This is best done from the **Front** view.

3. With everything closed, it is time to record our first keyframe. With all the bones selected, press *I* to open the **Insert Keyframe Menu** and select the **Location** option. This will record all of the initial positions of each of the pieces of the Artifact in frame 1. In Unreal, this will be used as our reference pose or starting pose:

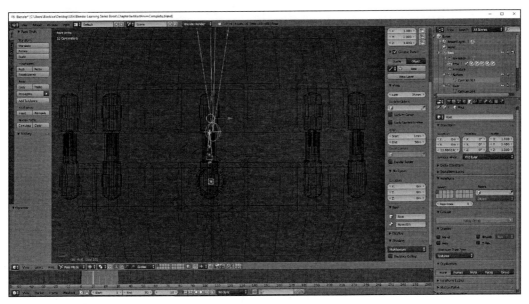

Animating the pistons extending

4. Now move the time slider in the **Timeline** at the bottom of the screen to frame 10. Next, deselect the bone that controls the bottom section. Move the other bones up until the bottom section of the piston has reached full extension. Press *I* and record the new location of the bones:

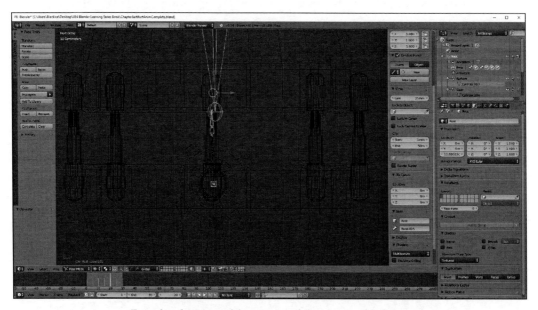

Extend each section of the piston and then create a keyframe

5. Move the time slider to frame 20 and deselect the bone that controls the bottom layer of the piston. Move the remaining bones up until the middle layer of the piston is at full extension. Press *I* and record the new location of the bones:

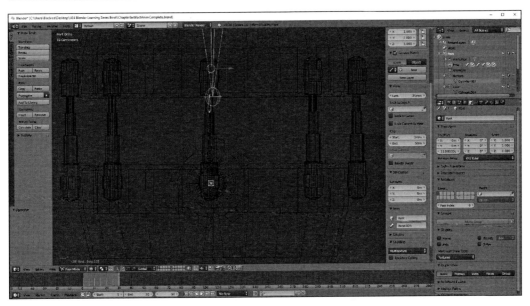

The pistons at full extension

6. Last move! Move the time slider to frame `30` and deselect the bone that controls the middle layer of the piston. Move the remaining bones up until the top layer of the piston is at full extension. Press *I* and record the new location of the bones.

7. Slide the time slider back and forth across our keyframes and watch as the Artifact opens and closes. Make some monster noises as you do so.

8. With our pistons working, let's add some rotation to the gear. Slide the time slider to frame `5` and rotate the bone that controls it `45` degrees by pressing *R*, typing in `45`, and pressing *Enter*. Press *I* and select the **Rotation** option from the menu. Slide the time slider to frame `10` and repeat. Repeat this process until you have recorded new rotation keyframes for the gear bone and five frame intervals.

9. Slide the time slider back and forth over the whole animation and test how it looks.

Summary

We have just brought the Artifact to life! In game terms, the Artifact will take 1 second to open. Feel free to adjust the keyframes in the Dope Sheet if you would like the process to take more or less time. More time might be appropriate if we wanted to created tension and fear. Less time might work better if we want to surprise the player or leave them little time to react to what happens next. Go with your gut and adjust the keyframes to meet your game's needs. It is also possible to use this same process to animate the tentacle to give our asset more unholy life!

In this chapter, we looked at the process of animating using the tools available inside Blender. We learned how to use keyframes and adjust those keyframes using the Dope Sheet. Finally, we created an armature of bones for the Artifact, which we were able to use to create an opening animation for when the player encounters it in Unreal. In the next chapter, we will import everything into Unreal and put all of these pieces together. We will then finish the project with a bang by having the player blow the Artifact up!

9
Bang Bang – Let's Make It Explode

Here we are. The end. Together, we've begun the process of creating a pretty good game idea. We started with a basic level that, when it comes right down to it, is simply two rooms connected by a hallway with a simple crate. From humble beginnings, our game has grown, as have our skills. Our simple cargo ship leads the player to a larger space station level. This level includes scripted events to move the story along and a game asset that looks great and animates. However, we are not done. How do we end our journey? We blow things up, that's how!

In this chapter, we will cover the following topics:

- Using class blueprints to bring it all together
- Creating an explosion using sound effects
- Adding particle effects

Creating a class blueprint to tie it all together

We begin with the first step of any type of digital destruction, creation. Over the last few chapters, we have created a disturbing piece of ancient technology. The Artifact stands as a long forgotten terror weapon of another age, somehow brought forth by an unknown power. But we know the truth. That unknown power is us, and we are about to import all that we need to implement the Artifact on the deck of our space station. Players beware!

Take a look at the end result:

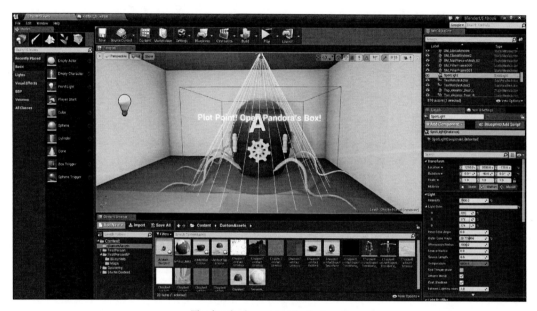

The finished asset inside the level!

To get started, we will need to import the Artifact body, the tentacle, and all of the texture maps from **Substance Painter**. Let's start with exporting the main body of the Artifact.

1. In Blender, open our file with the complete Artifact. The FBX file format will allow us to export both the completed 3D model and the animations we created, all in a single file.
2. Select the Artifact only. Since it is now bound to the skeleton we created, the bones and the geometry should all be one piece.
3. Now press *Alt + S* to reset the scale of our game asset. Doing this will make sure that we won't have any weird scaling problems when we import the Artifact into Unreal.
4. Head to the **File** menu and select **Export**. Choose **FBX** as our file format.
5. On the first tab of the export menu, select the checkbox for **Selected Objects**. This will make sure that we get just the Artifact and not the tentacle.
6. On the **Geometries** tab, change the **Smoothing** option to **Faces**.
7. Name your file and click **Export**!

Alright, we now have the latest version of the Artifact exported as an FBX. Now that we have exported a few things over the course of the book, do you feel like you have a good handle on the process? Try repeating the process with the tentacle now.

 Once you are done working through all the exercises in this book, don't just put it on a shelf. With all the different processes described in its pages, it makes a great reference!

Time to bring up Unreal. Open the game engine and load our space station level. It's been a while since we've taken a look at it, and there is no doubt in my mind that you've probably thought of improvements and new sections you would love to add. Don't forget them! Just set them aside for now. Once we get our game assets in there and make them explode, you will have plenty of time to add things.

Time to import into Unreal!

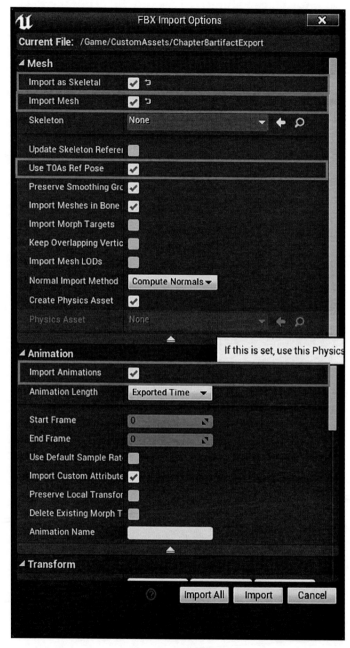

Importing a skeletal mesh is a bit different than a static mesh

1. Before we begin importing our pieces, let's create a folder to hold our custom assets. Click on the **Content** folder in the **Content Browser** and then right-click on it. At the top of the menu that appears, select **New Folder** and name it `CustomAssets`. It's very important not to use spaces or special characters (besides the underscore).

2. Select our new folder and click **Import**. Select the **Artifact FBX** file.

3. At the top of the **Import** menu, make sure **Import as Skeletal** and **Import Mesh** are selected. Now click the small arrow at the bottom of the section to open the advanced options. Lastly, turn on the check box to tell Unreal to use **To As Reference Pose**. A **Reference Pose** is the starting point for any animations associated with a skeletal mesh.

4. Next, take a look at the **Animation** section of the menu. Turn on **Import Animations** to tell Unreal to bring in our open animation for the Artifact.

5. Once all that is done, it's time to click **Import**!

Unreal will create a **Skeletal Mesh**, an **Animation**, a **Physics Asset**, and a **Skeleton** asset for the Artifact. Together, these pieces make up a fully functioning skeletal mesh that can be used within our game.

Importing the Artefact will create four important assets: the Skeletal Mesh, the Animation, the Physics Asset, and the Skeleton

Take a moment and repeat the process for the tentacle, again being careful to make sure to export only selected objects from Blender. Next, we need to import all of our texture maps from Substance Painter:

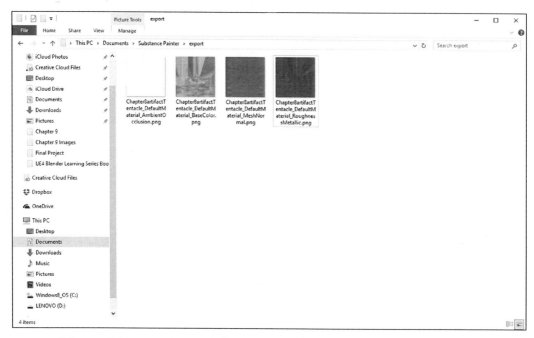

Substance Painter stores its exported texture maps in Documents\Substance Painter\export

In the last part of *Chapter 6, Monster Assets – The Level Totally Needs One of These*, we exported several texture maps for the Artifact that should be still be in the `Export` folder:

1. Locate the `Export` folder for **Substance Painter**. By default it is located in the **Documents** folder, under **Substance Painter**, and finally under **Export**.

2. Head back into Unreal and then bring up the **Export** folder from your computer's task bar. Click and drag each of the texture maps we need into the **Content Browser**. Unreal will import them automatically.

3. Time to set them all up as a usable material! Right-click in the **Content Browser** and select **Material** from the **Create Basic Asset** section of the menu. Name the material Artifact_MAT. This will open a **Material Editor** window:

The Material Editor window

The **Material Editor** works similar to programming in Blueprint and uses a similar node structure. The large node in the center represents the final result.

Tip: Creating materials and shaders for video games is an art form all its own. Here I will talk about creating materials in basic terms, but I would encourage you to check out the Unreal documentation, open up some of the existing materials in the Starter Content folder, and begin exploring this highly versatile tool.

4. So we need to add our textures to our new material. An easy way to add texture maps to any material is to click and drag them from the **Content Browser** into the **Material Editor**. This will create a node called a **Texture Sample**, which can plug into the different sockets on the main material node.

5. Now to plug in each map. Drag a wire from each of the white connections on the right side of each **Texture Sample** to its appropriate slot on the main material node. The **Metallic** and **Roughness** texture sample will be plugged into two slots on the main node.

6. Let's preview the result. Back in the **Content Browser**, select the **Artifact**. Then, in the **Preview Window** of the **Material Editor**, select the small button on the far right that reads **Set the Preview Mesh based on the current Content Browser selection**.

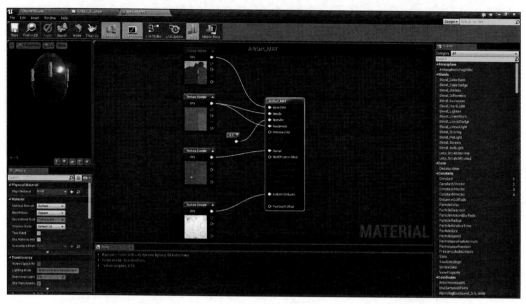

Each of the four maps we imported has a corresponding socket on the main material node

7. The material has come out just a bit too shiny. The large amount of shine given off by the material is called the specular highlight and is controlled by the **Specular** connection on the main material node. If we check the documentation, we can see that this part of the node accepts a value between 0 and 1. How might we do this? Well, the **Material Editor** has a **Constant** node that allows us to input a number and then plug that in wherever we may need it. This will work perfectly! Search for a **Constant** in the search box of the **Palette**, located on the right side of the **Material Editor**. Drag it into the area with your other nodes and head over to the **Details** panel. In the **Value** field, try different values between 0 and 1 and preview the result. I ended up using 0.1. Save your changes.

Time to try it out on our Artifact!

In the Skeletal Mesh editor, assign our new material to the Artefact in the Mesh Details panel

8. Double-click on the **Skeletal Mesh** to open the **Skeletal Mesh** editor window. On the left-hand side, look for the **LOD0** section of the menu. This section has an option to add a material (I have highlighted it in the preceding image). Head back to the content browser and select our **Artifact_MAT** material. Now select the small arrow in the **LOD0** box to apply the selection to the Artifact.

How does it look? Too shiny? Not shiny enough? Feel free to adjust our **Constant** node in the material node until you are able to get the result you want. When you are happy, repeat the process for the tentacle. We will import it as a static mesh (since it doesn't have any animations) and create a material for it made out of the texture maps we created in **Substance Painter**.

Now we will use a **Class Blueprint** for final assembly.

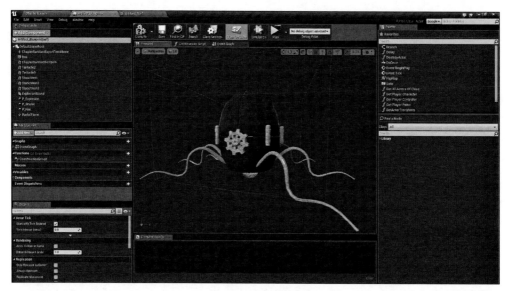

The Artefact Class Blueprint

Class Blueprints are a form of standalone Blueprint that allows us to combine art assets with programming in an easy-to-use and, most importantly, reusable package. For example, the player is a class Blueprint as it combines the player character's Skeletal Mesh with Blueprint code to help the player move around:

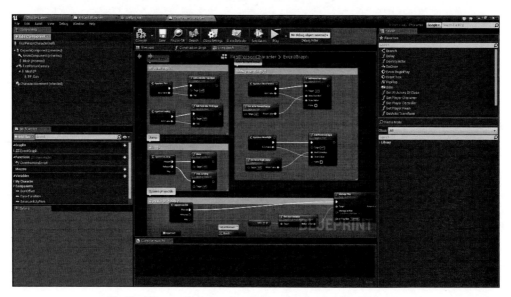

The First Person Character is a great example of a class Blueprint

So how and when might we use class Blueprints instead of just putting the code in the level Blueprint? The level blueprint is great for anything that is specific to just that level. Such things would include volcanoes on a lava-based level, or spaceships in the background of our space station level. Class Blueprints work great for building objects that are self-contained and repeatable, such as doors, enemies, or power-ups. These types of item would be used frequently and would have a place in several levels of a game.

Let's create a class blueprint for the Artifact:

1. Click on the **Blueprints** button and select the **New Empty Blueprints** tab. This will open the **Pick Parent Class** menu. Since we are creating a prop, and not something that the player needs to control directly, select the **Actor Parent Class**.

2. The next screen will ask us to name our new class and for a location to save it to. I chose to save it in my **CustomAssets** folder and named it `Artifact_Blueprint`.

3. Welcome to the **Class Blueprint** editor:

The Class Blueprint editor has several panels in common with the other editors inside Unreal

4. Similar to other editor windows within Unreal, the **Class Blueprint** editor has both a **Details** panel and a **Palette**. However, there is a panel that is new to us. The **Components** panel contains a list of the art types that makes up a class Blueprint. These components are various pieces that make up the whole object. For our Artifact, this would include the main piece itself, any number of tentacles, and a collision box. Other components that can be added include particle emitters, audio, and even lights.

5. Let's add the **Artifact**. In the **Components** section, click the **Add Component** button and select **Skeletal Mesh** from the drop-down list. You can find it in the **Common** section. This adds a blank **Skeletal Mesh** to the viewport and the **Components** list. With it selected, check out the **Details** panel. In the **Mesh** section is an area to assign the skeletal mesh you wish it to be. Back in the **Content Browser**, select the **Artifact**. Lastly, back in the **Details** panel of the **Blueprint Editor**, click the small arrow next to the **Skeletal Mesh** option to assign the **Artifact**. It should now appear in the viewport.

6. Back to the **Components** list. Let's add a **Box Collision**. Click **Add Component** and select **Box Collision** from the **Collision** section of the menu:

Select the Add Component button and choose Box Collision from the dropdown

7. Click it and in the **Details** panel, increase the **Box Extents** to a size that would allow the player to enter within its bounds. I used 180 for *x*, *y*, and *z*.

8. Repeat the last few steps and add the tentacles to the Artifact using the **Add Component** menu. We will use the **Static Mesh** option. The design calls for three, but add more if you like.

9. Time to give this class Blueprint a bit of programming. We want the player to be able to walk up to the Artifact and press the *E* key to open it.

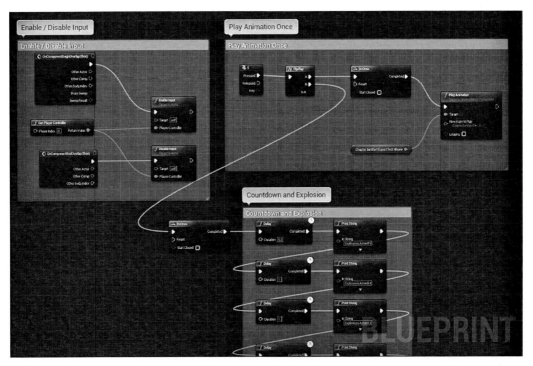

Programming the Artefact

10. When we created a similar type of control for the elevator back in *Chapter 2, Starting Our First Project*, we used a **Gate** to control the flow of information through the Blueprint. However, **Gates** don't function the same within class Blueprints, so we require a slightly different approach. The first step in the process is to use the **Enable Input** and **Disable Input** nodes, to allow the player to use input keys when they are within our box collision. Using the search box located within our **Palette**, grab an **Enable Input** and a **Disable Input**. Now we need to add our trigger events. Click on the **Box** variable within the **Variable** section of the **My Blueprint** panel. This changes the **Details** panel to display a list of all the **Events** that can be created for this component. Click the **+** button next to the **OnComponentBeginOverlap** and the **OnComponentEndOverlap** events. Connect the **OnComponentBeginOverlap** event to the **Enable Input** node, and the **OnComponentEndOverlap** event to the **Disable Input** node.

11. Next, create an event for the player pressing the *E* key by searching for it and dragging it in from the **Palette**.

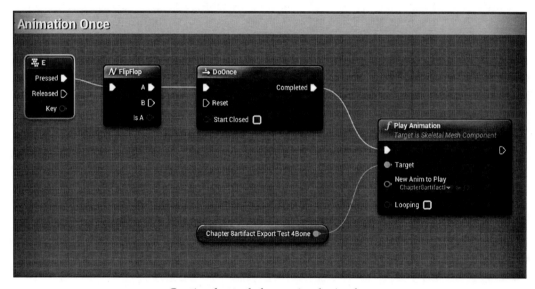

Creating the toggle for opening the Artefact

12. To that, we will add a **Do Once** node. This node works similar to a **Gate** in that it restricts the flow of information through the network, but it does allow the action to happen once before closing. This will make it so the player can press *E* to open the Artifact, but the animation will only play once. Without it, a player can press *E* as many times as they want, playing the animation over and over again. It's fun for a while, since it makes it look like a mouth trying to eat you, but it's not our original intention (I might have spent some time pressing it repeatedly and laughing hysterically). **Do Once** can be easily found in the **Palette**. Lastly, we will need a **Play Animation** node. There are two versions, so be sure to grab this node from the **Skeletal Mesh** section of your search so that its target is **Skeletal Mesh Component**. Connect the input **E** event to the **Do Once** node, and the **Do Once** node to the **Play Animation**.

13. One last thing to complete this sequence. We need to set the target and animation to play on the **Play Animation** node. So the target will be our **Skeletal Mesh** component. Click on the **Artifact** component in the **Components** list, drag it into the **Blueprint** window, and plug that into the **Target** on our **Play Animation**. Lastly, click the dropdown under the **New Anim to Play** option on the **Play Animation** node and select our animation of the Artifact opening. We're done!

Let's save all of our files and test this out. Drag the **Artifact** into our space station and position it in the Import/Export Broker's shop. Build the level and then drop it in and test it. Did it open? Does it need more tentacles? Debug and refine it until it is exactly what you want.

Using sound effects

Now that we have the Artifact, tentacles, and animation working in our level, we could just stop there and call it done, right? We could, but wouldn't it be more fun give the player an opportunity to strike back at the dark power that has taken over our space station? Let's blow that Artifact up!

Before we just jump right in, we need to plan this out a bit. This will help us be able to think through the programming logic of the blueprint sequence and plan out how to build the explosion. So what goes into a great video game explosion? Well there has to be sound. Without a good solid explosion sound, any attempt at this will fall flat. We also need fire, smoke, and chunks to really make it shine. There has to be some type of instigating event, such as time, player interaction, or damage. Lastly, a rough sequence of events might be event, sound, explosion particle, smoke particle, delete object, and chunky particle. This way the smoke, explosion, and chunky particle effect will cover when we delete the exploding asset. Just our luck, Unreal has most of those pieces in the `Starter Content` folder!

Let's start prepping for our explosion within our class Blueprint by adding the sound effects and setting them to trigger when we need them.

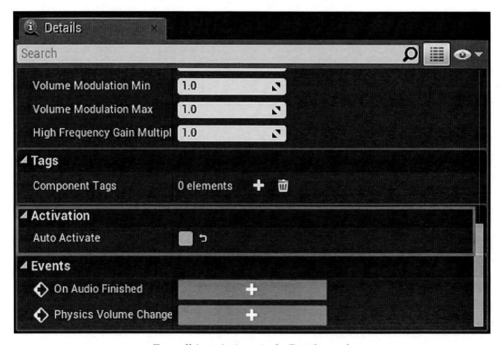

Turn off Auto Activate in the Details panel

Sounds can be imported into Unreal in the same we have imported other assets. If you feel the Starter Content sounds don't fit for your explosion, feel free to search for `Royalty Free` sounds. These are sounds that can be used in your projects for either free or a small upfront fee. `Royalty Free` means that beyond the initial payment, there is no further payment required.

1. Adding sounds to our class blueprint is similar to adding any other type of **component** and can provide some real depth to our explosion. In the **Class Blueprint** editor, click the **Add Component** button and select **Audio** from the list. Next, with the audio component selected, head to the **Details** panel and find the **Sound** option. Here, you will find a field where we can assign a **Sound Wave** or a **Sound Cue** by selecting it in the **Content Browser** and then clicking the small arrow. Alternately, you can select the sound you want to use before clicking the **Add Component** button, and Unreal will add the selected sound. Let's make this one the **Explosion Cue**. To make sure it only goes off when we want it to, select it and head to the **Details** panel. Find the **Auto Activate** option and turn it off.

Tip: The difference between a Sound Wave and a Sound Cue is very similar to the differences between Textures and Materials. Sound Waves make up Sound Cues, along with a few special Blueprint nodes. Double-click the **Explosion Cue** and take a look!

2. Time to add on a bit to our Artifact's programming! I know, everyone gets excited about this part. Let's add a bit of fun to our explosion and add a countdown clock.

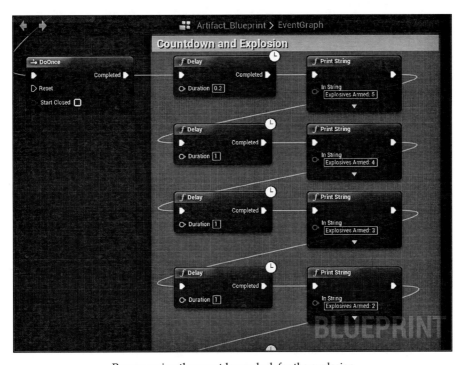

Programming the countdown clock for the explosion

3. We will branch this functionality off the event on pressing *E* using a **Flip Flop** node.

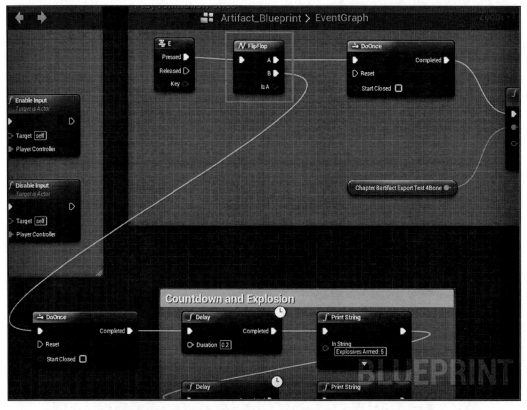

Connect the countdown to branch B on the Flip Flop we created earlier

4. Back in *Chapter 2, Starting Our First Project*, we used a **Flip Flop** node to control our cargo elevator. Essentially, the node will do branch **A** and then branch **B**, alternating between them. We will use it to allow the *E* key to first open the Artifact and then allow the player to place a bomb and start a countdown. Head over to the search box in the **Palette** panel, search for **Flip Flop**, and drag one into the **Blueprint** window. Break the connection between the **E** event and the **Do Once** node, and connect it up as shown in the preceding image.

5. Let's create the countdown. For this feature, we will use the **Print String** node to print out a 5-second countdown before we trigger our explosion sound.

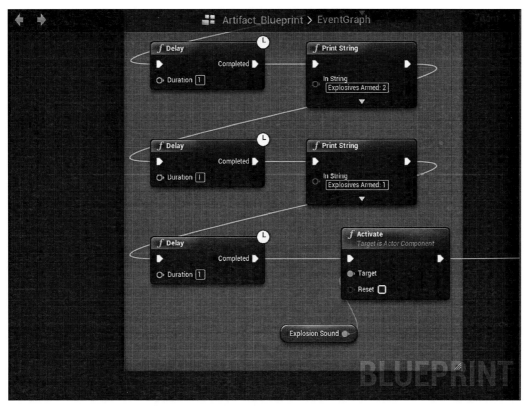

Program the Print String nodes in the countdown

6. To start, we will need a **Delay** node and a **Print String** node. Both of these can be found using the search box in the **Palette** panel. For the **Delay** node, go ahead and leave the **Duration** at 0.2. Change the **In String** option on the **Print String** node to read Explosives Armed: 5. Left-click and drag to select both of these nodes and copy/paste them. On these new nodes, change the **Duration** on the delay to 1.0 and the **In String** on the **Print String** node to Explosives Armed: 4. Repeat the process three more times to complete the countdown. The last node in the sequence is the **Activate** node. Since we turned off the **Auto Activate** option on our **Explosion Cue**, this node will activate the component and play the sound. With all of our pieces now in the **Blueprint** window, connect them together just like the preceding image.

7. Save and compile our class Blueprint. Save your level and press **Play** to test it!

Now that we have our sound effect working, there are only a few move steps to complete our explosion. However, there are a lot of other opportunities for using sounds in this Blueprint. For example, we could add an opening sound to the Artifact, or some eerie music to play while it's open. Experiment and see how you can use sound to further enhance the mood!

Using particle effects

The sounds of our explosion are all in place and the Artifact is ready for destruction! To finish our explosion, we are going to need some particle effects. We used various particle effects back in *Chapter 5, Taking This Level Up a Notch*, to enhance our scripted events at the security checkpoint and the elevator. Here we will use an explosion, fire, and smoke to enhance the destruction effect and mask when we delete the different components of the Artifact. Let's take a look:

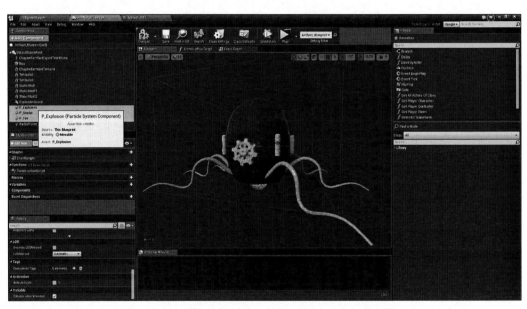

Add an explosion particle, a fire particle, and a smoke particle to the
Components list. Be sure to turn off Auto Activate!

To our already extensive list of components, we will add explosion, fire, and smoke particle emitters. Add each emitter, just like we added our sound, and then select each one and disable the **Auto Activate** option in the **Details** panel. We will use the Blueprint node **Activate** to turn those back on later.

Create two separate Class Blueprints for the top and bottom pieces of the Artefact. We will use them as shrapnel in the explosion

The last piece necessary to really make this explosion great is to add flying chunks! When a solid object explodes, parts of it tend to go flying in all directions. We will simulate this by having our Blueprints spawn versions of the bottom and the top of the Artifact, with physics enabled, which will fly around and stay in the level after the rest of the Artifact has been destroyed:

1. This will require us to head back to Blender and export versions of our **Top** and **Bottom** as separate FBX files. Open our **Blender** file and select the **Top** of the Artifact. Head up to the **File** menu and head to the **FBX Export** screen. Turn on the **Selected Objects** option so that only the **Top** is exported. Also, head to the **Geometries** tab and change the **Smoothing** option to **Face**. Name it something unique and export! Rinse and repeat for our **Bottom** piece and prepare to import them into Unreal.

2. Import both of our new FBX files into Unreal as static meshes, and apply our artifact material to them. You will notice that even though we did not import the whole model, our material still works perfectly. This is because the UV maps for each piece are still the same, whether we use the whole Artifact or only parts.

3. Time to create two new class Blueprints. Create a class `Blueprint` for each new static mesh by clicking the **Blueprint** button, selecting **New Empty Blueprint Class**, and selecting **Actor** as the **Parent Class**. I named mine `ArtifactTopChunk` and `ArtifactBotChunk`.

4. In each Blueprint, add the appropriate static mesh as a component. Just add it in; there is no need to move it. This way, they will be in the exact position we need them to be when we use our Blueprint to spawn them.

5. Now we need to make a couple of changes to their **Details**.

Apply physics to our flying pieces

6. For each of our new Blueprints, click the component and find the **Physics** section in the **Details** panel. First, turn on **Simulate Physics**. This will allow our objects to bounce around and be affected by gravity and outside forces. Next, turn on **Mass in Kg**. Normally, Unreal will calculate a physics object's mass, based on its size in the level. Both of our pieces come in at around 500 kg, not very good for being flying shrapnel. Turning on **Mass in Kg** allows us to override Unreal's best guess and fill in whatever value we wish for its weight. I used 50 kg, but feel free to use whatever you wish. It can always be adjusted later. Be sure to do this for both the **Top** and **Bottom** Artifact chunks.

Time to finish the Artifact's demise. Back in the Artifact class Blueprint, there is one more **Component** to add to our setup. To make our **Top** and **Bottom** chunks fly, we will use a **Radial Impulse** component to simulate the force of the blast. Add the **Radial Impulse** through the **Add Component** menu and find the **Radial Force Component** section of the **Details** panel. The radius that the impulse will affect is shown in the viewport as a light blue sphere. Increase the size of the **Radius** property until it covers the entire Artifact. I used 250. Also in the **Details** panel, find the **Impulse** section and increase the **Impulse Strength**. I used 2000. Lastly, make sure to turn on the **Impulse Vel Change** option. This option makes sure that the 2000 units of force are applied directly as a velocity change. This will guarantee to throw our chunks a good distance and maybe even the player!

Time for the last bit of programming! Let's take a look:

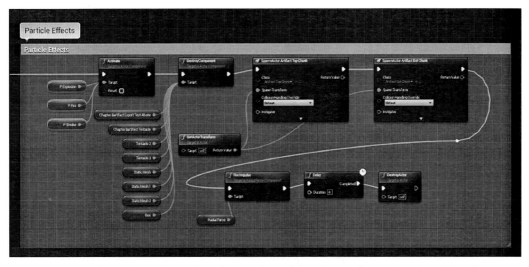

Activate the explosion, fire, and smoke particles and then destroy the mesh portions. We will then use two Spawn Actor From Class nodes to spawn our Top and Bottom chunks. Finally, fire the Radial Impulse to watch them bounce!

There isn't too much to this final section. We will use a second **Activate** node off the end of the countdown section to activate all of our particle effects. Then use a **Destroy Component** node to get rid of the components that would be destroyed in the blast. Next, we will use two **Spawn Actor From Class** nodes to spawn our two chunks, before finally using a **Fire Impulse** node to throw them away from the blast. Lastly, we will **Delay** 4 seconds before using a **Destroy Actor** to clean up the whole thing. Start by using the search box in the **Palette** to grab the **Activate** node. Place it at the end of the countdown sequence and connect it to the **Activate** node we used to play our sound cue. The **Activate** node needs one or more **Targets** to know what to turn on. From the **Components** panel grab the **P_Explosion**, **P_Smoke**, and **P_Fire** components and drag them into the Blueprint. Connect these to **Target** node on the **Activate** node.

Next in line is the **Destroy Component** node. We will use this node to delete everything that would be destroyed in the explosion. Connect it to our **Activate** node and set its **Targets** to be the Artifact, the collision box, and all the tentacles.

Time for **Spawn Actor From Class**! This great node allows us to use Blueprints to spawn other class Blueprints, but requires a few more parameters than **Activate** or **Destroy Component**.

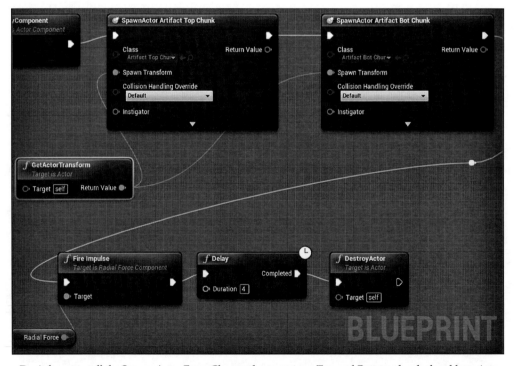

Don't forget to tell the Spawn Actor From Class nodes to use our Top and Bottom chunk class blueprints

Place the **Spawn Actor From Class** node next to the **Destroy Component** node and link them. The first thing we need to tell it is what class to spawn. Click the drop-down box and select the bottom **Artifact** chunk. The second thing it needs to know is where to spawn. This can be done by plugging a **Get Actor Transform** node (found using the search box in the **Palette**) into the **Spawn Transform** option. Now we are set to spawn! Repeat this step to set up a **Spawn Actor From Class** node for the top **Artifact** chunk.

Now fire that **Radial Impulse** and make this a true explosion!

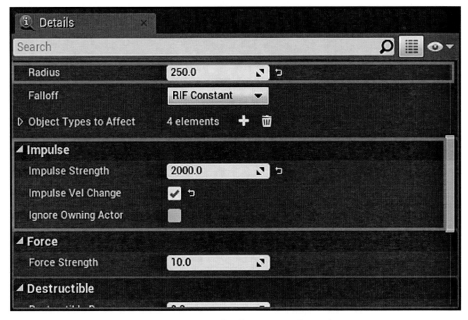

Use these settings for the Fire Impulse node

The node we need to use is **Fire Impulse**. The only thing this node needs is a **Target**. Grab our **Radial Impulse** component from the **Components** panel and plug it in.

To wrap things up we just need to do a little bit of housekeeping. At the end of this sequence, add a **Delay** and a **Destroy Actor** node. The **Delay** will be set to 4.0 seconds to give our sounds time to play, and the **Destroy Actor** will have **Self** as a **Target**. This will remove all of the class Blueprint from the level. However, it will leave the exploded chunks behind. Even though we used a class Blueprint to spawn them, they are separate Actors and will not be deleted when the rest of the class Blueprint deletes itself.

Make sure the sequence is connected up in order and test it. You should have a satisfying explosion that throws pieces of the Artifact around. If the player is too close, it will even throw them backward!

Explosions are so much fun to make and can be a great way to add a bit of action to any experience, but if you had fun building this sequence, you don't need to stop here. Try adding more explosion particle effects, or adding the tentacles as chunks for added effect.

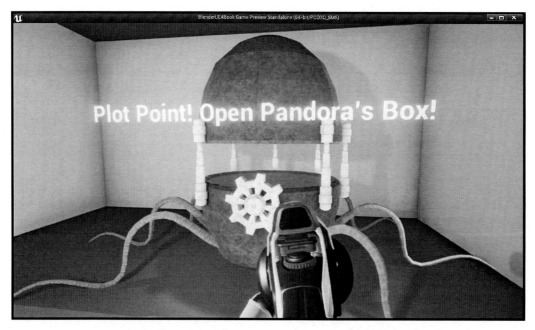

The final result! I hope you all had as much fun as I did!

How oddly satisfying was that?! There is just something about building something amazing for a video game and then allowing our player to blow it up. With our game asset now properly set up, we can place it in our space station level and use it as a goal to drive our gameplay forward. In this chapter, we went through the process of bringing our fully textured and animated Artifact in to Unreal and setting it up to look great in the level. We used a class Blueprint setup to assemble the pieces and created a way for the player to interact with it, causing it open. We then added some additional components and programming that allowed the player to start a countdown and blow up our game asset in a fine display of fire, smoke, and flying chunks.

And with that, we are done! Congratulations on finishing the book! What you have created is a great skeleton of a game that can be expanded on to create something amazing and uniquely your own. You have two whitebox levels that can be filled with your own custom art created in Blender. You have two game assets that can be further customized to fit your game's specific needs. I would strongly encourage you to properly finish each of these levels and to keep practicing and polishing your skills. Become the game designer or game artist that you want to be and I truly look forward to playing your unique games in the future!

Stick with it and game on!

Index

Symbols

3D asset
  setting up 79-85
  using 79-85

A

animation
  handling 185-187
  tools, using 200-203
asset
  designing 114, 115
Autodesk 3ds Max 1
Average Island Scale 149

B

Blender
  animation, handling 185-187
  Foundation 1
  installing 2, 3
  multiple shapes, using within 119-122,
    134-142
  object, exporting from 71-75
  suite of animation tools, using 200-203
  URL 2
blocking volumes 89
Blueprints
  used, for adding interactive elements 31-41
Bridge Edge Loops tool 118

C

class blueprint
  creating 206-214

creating, for artifact 215-219
complex objects
  average island scale 149
  pack islands 150
  seams, creating 146
  Smart UV Project, using 150, 151
  stitch 148
  unwrapping 145
  unwrap tool 147
Content Browser
  used, for start building level 15-28
cubes
  unwrapping 152, 153
Custom Marking Seams
  about 151
  cubes, unwrapping 152, 153
  cylinders, unwrapping 154-164
cylinders
  unwrapping 154-164

F

FBX 75

G

game asset
  making 44-46
  UV unwrapping 60-65

I

interactive elements
  adding, Blueprints used 3141
  adding, Triggers used 31-41
interface
  exploring 3-6

K

keyframes
  rigging 188-199
  using 188-199
Knife tool 117

L

level
  complex level, planning 87-89
  design, principles 93-95
  playtesting 41
  whiteboxing, for better asset creation 89-92
  win conditions 109-111
light
  using 28-31

M

maps
  different maps, used for creating realistic
    look 165-184
  diffuse maps 165
  normal map 167, 168
  specular map 166
modes
  working with 8
multiple shapes
  using, within Blender 119-142

O

object
  exporting, from Blender 71-75
  importing, into Unreal 76-79

P

pack islands 150
parenting 198
particle effects
  using 224-231
Physically Based Rendering (PBR) 168
polygon modeling
  basic tools, using 46-57
project
  working with 8, 9

S

scripting
  advanced scripting techniques 95-109
settings
  customizing 6, 7
Smart UV Project 145
  using 150, 151
sound effects
  using 219-224
stitch 148
Subdivide tool 116
Substance Painter
  about 171
  URL 69, 171
Substance Painter Texturing 173

T

texturing
  techniques 66-69
tools
  about 115
  Bridge Edge Loops tool 118
  Knife tool 117
  Subdivide tool 116
  Triangulate modifier tool 118, 119
Triggers
  used, for adding interactive elements 31-41

U

Unreal
  object, importing into 77-79
Unreal Engine
  about 1, 4, 9-11
  URL 9
unwrap tool 147
UV mapping
  about 60
  using 57-59